1 MONTH OF
FREE
READING

at
www.ForgottenBooks.com

By purchasing this book you are eligible for one month membership to ForgottenBooks.com, giving you unlimited access to our entire collection of over 1,000,000 titles via our web site and mobile apps.

To claim your free month visit:
www.forgottenbooks.com/free1374340

ISBN 978-1-397-32680-5
PIBN 11374340

For support please visit www.forgottenbooks.com

ANNOUNCEMENT

—— OF THE ——

College of Physicians and Surgeons

OF ONTARIO

FOR 1915 — 1916

REGISTRY OFFICE

COLLEGE OF PHYSICIANS & SURGEONS OF ONTARIO

170 University Avenue, Toronto

SEPTEMBER — 1915

THE ARMAC PRESS, LIMITED
Toronto

Request is made of the Members
of the College, that they read

The Red Ink Appeal-

The Council of the College of Physicians and Surgeons of Ontario, at its Annual Meeting this year, made provision for the issue of a new Register, at an early date.

Since the date of the issue of the last published Register (1907), there have been several hundred names added to the list of the licentiates of the College, so that the present Register does not in any sense represent its full membership, and, with each recurring year, witnessing further such additions, its value, for purposes of reference, becomes increasingly impaired.

In its book form, the Register is composed essentially of two parts, the first consisting of a copy of the Ontario Medical Act, the second comprising a list of the Members of the College (up to the date of publication), their names and addresses, their degrees and qualifications.

The College Counsel, Mr. H. S. Osler, K.C., will stand sponsor for the correctness of the copy of the Ontario Medical Act, with its various additions, alterations and amendments, as it will appear in the new issue of the Register.

The College Members must themselves, in the last analysis, be held responsible for the correctness of their own names and addresses, as these, in turn, will appear in the same Register. The Officers of the College, while using all available means to collect necessary data, relating thereto, must look to the Members for sympathetic co-operation, in the preparation of a Register, which, in detail, shall be, as far as possible, full and accurate.

It can never be absolutely so, possibly owing, in part at least, to that ethnic quality, inherent in many of the Members of the Profession, of seeking from time to time a new place of abode, but can through concerted effort on the part of those Members who are more sessile in this respect, be made of such relative value, as to quite justify any expenditure of energy directed to this end.

There is no field in which the exercise of the personal equation can have more room for play, than in this connection, and none in which less sacrifice is asked of those who are best qualified to contribute to efficiency of service. Such sacrifice, if that which ends in personal gain may be thus designated, is wholly trifling, and quite incommensurate with the benefits which must accrue from its exercise.

The licentiates of the College are aware that the College has a Register, and they know that the measure of its value is determined by the extent to which it is correct and up-to-date. They

CONTENTS

	PAGE
COUNCIL MEMBERSHIP	7-8
OFFICERS, EXAMINERS	9
STANDING COMMITTEES	10
PAST OFFICERS	11-13
ANNOUNCEMENT	14-15

REGULATIONS—

Matriculation	16
Curriculum	16
Registration of British Practitioners	19
Examinations, date, place and requirements of	20
Examinations, duties of Registrar and Board of Examiners....	21
Examinations—Rules governing Candidates	22
Fees	24

EXAMINATION PAPERS, 1914	26-29
EXAMINATION PAPERS, 1915	29-32
MEMBERS OF COLLEGE, BY EXAMINATION, SINCE DATE OF LAST REGISTER	33-55
MEMBERS, OTHERWISE THAN BY EXAMINATION, AND CERTAIN NAMES OMITTED FROM LAST REGISTER........	56-73
BY-LAWS	74-94

SPECIAL COUNCIL MEETING, DECEMBER, 1914—

Report of Credentials Committee	95
Election of Officers	96
Reciprocity 99, 103,	105
By-laws	101
Finance Committee's Report	106

CONTENTS—*Continued.*

ANNUAL MEETING, JUNE-JULY, 1915—

Election of Officers 109

Resignation of Registrar 110

Report re Standing Committees 111

Examination Returns 113

Reciprocity 117, 118, 128, 129

Special Licenses granted 117

Dominion Medical Council 120

Appointment of Registrar-Treasurer ....'.................... 122

Discipline Committee's Report 123, 124, 133, 134

Osteopaths, Chiropractors, etc, ...: 125, 136

Education Committee's Report 127

Finance Committee's Report 130

Property Committee's Report 137

Prosecutor's Report 139

Dr. Spankie's resolution, re care of disabled soldiers 145

Payments to Examiners, Committee and Council Members..... 147

Treasurer's Report 150

PAYMENTS TO EXAMINERS, COMMITTEE MEMBERS, COUN-
CIL MEMBERS 147-149

TREASURER'S REPORT 150-152

COUNCIL OF

The College of Physicians and Surgeons

OF ONTARIO

Territorial Representatives.

G. R. Cruickshank, M.D., Windsor, Ont. ....Division No. 1
G. M. Brodie, M.D., Woodstock, Ont. .... " 2
F. R. Eccles, London, Ont. .... " 3
A. T. Emmerson, M.D., Goderich, Ont. 4
J. J. Walters, M.D., Berlin, Ont. 5
S. McCallum, M.D., Thornbury, Ont. 6
H. S. Griffin, M.D., Hamilton, Ont. 7
E. T. Kellam, M.D., Niagara Falls, Ont. 8
R. H. Arthur, M.D., Sudbury, Ont. 9
A. D. Stewart, M.D., Fort William, Ont. 10
E. E. King, M.D., Toronto, Ont. 11
H. J. Hamilton, M.D., Toronto, Ont. 12
F. A. Dales, M.D., Stouffville, Ont. 13
T. W. H. Young, M.D., Peterboro, Ont. 14
T. S. Farncomb, M.D., Trenton, Ont. 15
W. Spankie, M.D., Wolfe Island, Ont. .... " 16
W. E. Crain, M.D., Crysler, Ont. 17
J. F. Argue, M.D., Ottawa, Ont. 18

Collegiate Representatives.

J. M. MacCallum, M.D., Toronto, Ont....University of Toronto
E. Ryan, M.D., Kingston, Ont..............Queen's University
A. J. Johnson, M.D., Toronto, Ont..University of Trinity College
R. Ferguson, M.D., London, Ont....Western University, London
Sir J. A. Grant, Ottawa, Ont........Ottawa University, Ottawa
W. L. T. Addison, M.D., Toronto, Ont..Victoria University, Tor.

Homoeopathic Representatives.

H. Becker, M.D. ....Toronto, Ontario
E. A. P. Hardy, M.D. ....Toronto, Ontario
C. E. Jarvis, M.D. ....London, Ontario
G. A. Routledge, M.D. ....Lambeth, Ontario
A. E. Wickens, M.D. ....Hamilton, Ontario

Medical Registration Office
of the

COLLEGE OF PHYSICIANS & SURGEONS OF ONTARIO
170 University Avenue, Toronto.

Office Hours—10 a.m. to 4 p.m.   Saturdays—10 to 12 a.m.
H. Wilberforce Aikins, Registrar-Treasurer,
Toronto, Ontario.

OFFICERS OF

The College of Physicians and Surgeons

OF ONTARIO

FOR 1915 AND 1916.

President
H. S. GRIFFIN, M.D., Hamilton, Ont.

Vice-President
EDMUND E. KING, M.D., Toronto, Ont.

Registrar-Treasurer
H. WILBERFORCE AIKINS, M.D., Toronto, Ont.

Prosecutor
JOHN FYFE, Toronto, Ont.

College Counsel
H. S. OSLER, K.C.

BOARD OF EXAMINERS, 1915-1916

Surgery
DR. E. SEABORN, London, Ont.
DR. P. STUART, Guelph, Ont.

Medicine
DR. W. T. CONNELL, Kingston, Ont.
DR. J. P. VROOMAN, Napanee, Ont.

Midwifery and Diseases of Women
DR. W. A. THOMSON, London, Ont.
DR. H. T. MACHELL, Toronto, Ont.

Homoeopathic Examiners
DR. W. A. McFALL, Toronto, Ont.
DR. G. L. HUSBAND, Hamilton, Ont.

STANDING COMMITTEES OF

The College of Physicians and Surgeons

OF ONTARIO
FOR 1915-1916

Complaints Committee
Dr. Ryan, Chairman.

Dr. Arthur.   Dr. Becker.   Dr. Farncomb.   Dr. S. McCallum.

Discipline Committee
Dr. Crain, Chairman.

Dr. Emmerson.   Dr. S. McCallum.   Dr. Wickens.

Education Committee
Dr. Ferguson, Chairman.

Dr. Addison.   Dr. Arthur.   Dr. Emmerson.
Dr. James MacCallum.   Dr. Ryan.   Dr. Spankie.   Dr. Stewart.
Dr. Wickens.

Executive Committee
Dr. Griffin.   Dr. King.   Dr. Hardy.

Finance Committee
Dr. James MacCallum, Chairman.

Dr. Hamilton.   Dr. Kellam.   Dr. Routledge.   Dr. Stewart.

Legislative Committee
Dr. Ryan, Chairman.

Dr. Addison.   Dr. Argue.   Dr. Arthur.   Dr. Cruickshank.
Dr. Griffin.   Dr. Hamilton.   Dr. Hardy.   Dr. Jarvis.
Dr. King.   Dr. Routledge.   Dr. Walters.

Printing Committee
Dr. Johnson, Chairman

Dr. Brodie.   Dr. Dales.   Dr. Farncomb.   Dr. Kellam.

Property Committee
Dr. Johnson, Chairman.

Dr. Argue.   Dr. Crain.   Dr. Routledge.   Dr. Walters.

Registration Committee
Dr. Cruickshank, Chairman.

Dr. Ferguson. Dr. Hamilton. Dr. Jarvis. Dr. Spankie.

Rules and Regulations Committee
Dr. Emmerson, Chairman.

Dr. Addison. Dr. Argue. Dr. Crain. Sir James Grant.

Dr. Hardy. Dr. Walters.

OFFICERS OF THE COLLEGE OF PHYSICIANS AND SURGEONS OF ONTARIO FROM 1866 TO 1915-1916.

PRESIDENTS.

```
 1—John R. Dickson ..........................................1866—1867
 2—John Turquand ...........................................1867—1868
 3—James A. Grant ..........................................1868—1869
 4—William Clark ...........................................1869—1870
 5—William H. Brouse .......................................1870—1871
 6—Chas. W. Coverton ....................June to December    1871
 7—Wiliam Clark ..........................†December 1871—1872
 8—J. F. Dewar .............................................1872—1873
 9—William Clark ...........................................1873—1874
10—M. Lavell ...............................................1874—1875
11—E. G. Edwards ...........................................1875—1876
12—Daniel Clark ............................................1876—1877
13—Daniel Clark ............................................1877—1878
14—D. Campbell .............................................1878—1879
15—J. D. Macdonald .........................................1879—1880
16—W. Allison ..............................................1880—1881
17—D. Bergin ...............................................1881—1882
18—J. L. Bray ..............................................1882—1883
19—G. Logan ................................................1883—1884
20—H. W. Day ...............................................1884—1885
21—D. Bergin ...............................................1885—1886
22—H. H. Wright ............................................1886—1887
23—G. Henderson ............................................1887—1888
24—J. H. Burns .............................................1888—1889
25—J. G. Cranston ..........................................1889—1890
26—V. H. Moore .............................................1890—1891
27—J. A. Williams ..........................................1891—1892
28—F. Fowler ...............................................1892—1893
29—Cl. T. Campbell .........................................1893—1894
30—D. L. Philip ............................................1894—1895
```

* The President, Vice-President, Treasurer and Registrar of the College are elected at the Annual Meeting of the Council, and hold office until their successors are elected.

† Dr. William Clark was elected December 19, 1871, at a special meeting of the Council in consequence of the resignation of Dr. C. W. Coverton.

31—W. T. Harris ....1895—1896
32—A. F. Rogers ....1896—1897
33—J. Thorburn ....1897—1898
34—L. Luton ....1898—1899
35—W. F. Roome ....1899—1900
36—W. Britton ....1900—1901
37—L. Brock ....1901—1902
38—W. J. H. Emory ....1902—1903
39—J. A. Robertson ....1903—1904
40—M. Sullivan ....1904—1905
41—A. A. Macdonald ....1905—1906
42—W. H. Moorehouse ....1906—1907
43—W. Spankie ....1907—1908
44—H. S. Glasgow ....1908—1909
45—E. A. P. Hardy ....1909—1910
46—J. Lane ....1910—1911
47—R. J. Gibson ....1911—1912
48—Edward Ryan ....1912—1913
49—M. O. Klotz ....1913—1914
50—James MacArthur ....1914—1915
51—H. S. Griffin ....1915—1916

VICE-PRESIDENTS.

1—Wm. H. Brouse ....1866—1870
2—Chas. W. Covernton ....1870—1871
3—James Hamilton ....1871—1872
4—D. Campbell ....1872—1873
5—John Muir ....1873—1874
6—E. G. Edwards ....1874—1875
7—E. M. Hodder ....1875—1876
8—D. Campbell ....1876—1877
9—D. Campbell ....1877—1878
10—A. Allison ....1878—1879
11—G. Logan ....1879—1880
12—D. Bergin ....1880—1881
13—J. L. Bray ....1881—1882
14—W. B. Geikie ....1882—1883
15—H. W. Day ....1883—1884
16—E. W. Spragge ....1884—1885
17—R. Douglas ....1885—1886
18—G. Henderson ....1886—1887
19—J. H. Burns ....1887—1888
20—J. G. Cranston ....1888—1889
21—V. H. Moore ....1889—1890
22—J. A. Williams ....1890—1891
23—F. Fowler ....1891—1892
24—C. T. Campbell ....1892—1893
25—D. L. Philip ....1893—1894
26—W. T. Harris ....1894—1895
27—A. F. Rogers ....1895—1896
28—J. Thorburn ....1896—1897
29—J. Henry ....1897—1898
30—W. F. Roome ....1898—1899
31—W. Britton ....1899—1900
32—W. W. Dickson ....1900—1901
33—W. J. H. Emory ....1901—1902
34—J. A. Robertson ....1902—1903
35—M. Sullivan ....1903—1904

36—A. A. Macdonald ....1904—1905
37—W. H. Moorehouse ....1905—1906
38—W. Spankie ....1906—1907
39—P. Stuart ....1907—1908
40—E. A. P. Hardy ....1908—1909·
41—J. Lane ....1909—1910
42—R. J. Gibson ....1910—1911
43—E. Ryan ....1911—1912
44—M. O. Klotz ....1912—1913
45—Jas. MacArthur ....1913—1914
46—H. S. Griffin ....1914—1915
47—E. E. King ....1915—1916

TREASURERS.

W. T. Aikins ....1866—1897
H. Wilberforce Aikins ....1897—1915

REGISTRARS AND SECRETARIES.

Henry Strange ....May 3, 1866—Sept. 2, 1872
Thomas Pyne ....Sept. 2, 1872—July 15, 1880
Robt. A. Pyne ....July 15, 1880—July 2, 1907
John L. Bray ....July 2, 1907—June 29, 1915

REGISTRAR-TREASURER.

H. Wilberforce Aikins 1915

College of Physicians and Surgeons
OF ONTARIO

Announcement for the Academic Year
1915-1916

"The College of Physicians and Surgeons of Ontario" is the name adopted by the Medical Profession of the Province of Ontario in its corporate capacity. Every legally qualified medical practitioner in the Province is a member of this College. It is not an institution for the teaching of medicine.

The Medical Profession of Ontario was first incorporated under this name by an Act of Parliament of Canada, passed in 1866. This Act was subsequently repealed by the Legislature of Ontario in 1869, and now the affairs of the Profession in this Province are regulated by an Act passed in 1874 (37 Vic.,-Cap. 30), commonly known as the "Ontario Medical Act," and further amended in 1887, 1891, 1893, 1895, 1902, 1905, and 1914-1915.

By this Act, the "Council of the College of Physicians and Surgeons of Ontario" is empowered and directed to enact by-laws for the regulation of all matters connected with medical education; for the admission and enrolment of students of medicine; for determining from time to time the curriculum of the studies to be pursued by them, and to appoint a Board of Examiners, before whom all candidates must pass a satisfactory examination before they can be enrolled as members of the College, and thus be legally qualified to practise their profession in the Province of Ontario.

The Council, moreover, has power and authority conferred upon it by this Act to fix the terms upon which practitioners of medicine, duly qualified in other countries, may be admitted as members of the College of Physicians and Surgeons of Ontario, this being the only mode in which they can become legally entitled to practice their profession in this Province.

For the information and guidance of students of medicine, the Profession, and the public generally, the Council, in conformity with the Ontario Medical Act, hereby promulgates for the year 1915-1916 the Regulations which herein follow, repealing all others heretofore in force.

All changes in the medical curriculum shall take effect at the next ensuing annual examinations.

Regulations for 1915-1916

SECTION I.

Matriculation.

Every one desirous of being registered as a matriculated student in the Register of this College, except as hereinafter provided, shall be required to pay a fee of twenty-five dollars and to conform to the following regulations:

Any one of the following credentials will be accepted:

1. A certificate of having graduated in Arts or Science in any university of His Majesty's Dominions, or any other university approved of by this Council.

2. A certificate from the Registrar of any chartered Canadian University conducting a full Arts course, that the holder thereof has passed the examination conducted at the end of the first year in Arts by such university.

3. A certificate of having passed the joint university senior matriculation examination in Arts as conducted by the Education Department of Ontario.

4. A certificate of having passed the Senior Arts matriculation conducted by any chartered university of Canada.

5. A certificate of having passed the joint university examination for junior matriculation in Arts conducted by the Education Department of Ontario.

Matriculation must be registered in the manner prescribed by the Council, preliminary to entrance upon medical studies.

The Registrar shall send to each High School and Collegiate Institute in Ontario, a printed copy of the regulations governing the matriculation requirements of this Council with the request that such be posted in the High School or Collegiate Institute.

SECTION II.

Curriculum.

1. Every student must spend a period of five years in actual professional studies, except as hereinafter provided; and the prescribed period of studies shall include four winter sessions of eight months each, and a fifth, or final year, to be devoted to clinical work.

The Registrar of this Council shall be required to exact from each candidate a certificate from his College Registrar, that he has attended lectures for a full term of eight months in each session, and further that such certificate must show that the candidate has attended not less than 80 per cent. of such lectures, including hospital and laboratory work.

2. Graduates in Arts or Science of any college or university recognized by the Council shall be permitted to present themselves for their examination in four years, provided that during such course two years have been spent in the course of physics, chemistry, biology and physiology, and examinations passed in these subjects while taking said university course.

3. Every student must attend the undermentioned course in a University, College or School of Medicine approved of by the Council.

Certificates must be presented for the full number of Clinical Lectures required.

Anatomy—Two courses of eight months each in descriptive and practical anatomy.

Each student will be required to prove that he has carefully dissected the entire adult human body.

Medical and Surgical Anatomy—One course of eight months.

Physiology—Two courses of eight months each.

Histology—One course of eight months.

Chemistry—Two courses of eight months each.

Medical Physics—One course of four months.

Materia Medica, Pharmacy and Pharmacology—Two courses of four months each.

Medicine—Two courses of eight months each.

Clinical Medicine—Two courses of eight months each.

Surgery—Two courses of eight months each.

Clinical Surgery—Two courses of eight months each.

Midwifery—Two courses of eight months each.

Gynecology—One course of eight months.

Pathology and Bacteriology—Two courses of eight months each.

Diseases of Children—One course of six months.

Therapeutics—One course of six months, including Medical Electricity and Roentgen Rays.

Jurisprudence and Toxicology—One course of four months.

Diseases of the Eye, Ear, Nose and Throat—One course of four months.

Hygiene and Preventive Medicine—One course of four months.

Psychiatry—One course of two months.

4. In lieu of certificate of the fifth year of the Medical Course spent at an approved University, Hospital or Medical School, any one of the following will be accepted:

(a) Certificate of having performed duties of Interne for one year in a recognized hospital.

(Hospital recognized by Government and receiving Government allowance).

(b) Certificate of having spent one year as assistant to a regularly qualified practitioner.

(c) Certificates of having spent six months of fifth year as assistant to a regularly qualified practitioner, and other six months as Interne in a recognized hospital.

(d) The Post Graduate Public Health Degree conferred by University of Toronto and the Institute of Public Health affiliated with the Western University, London, and Queen's University, Kingston, comprising a year's laboratory training and field work.

N.B.—Certificates recognized by paragraphs (a), (b) and (c), when presented, must be accompanied by Affidavit on a recognized form, duly and properly executed by the person from whom the certificate is procured. Blank forms of these Certificates are obtainable from the Registrar.

The minimum requirements of clinical lectures by the staff of a recognized hospital or at a medical school are as follows:

(a) Twenty-five lectures or demonstrations in Surgery.

(b) Twenty-five lectures or demonstrations in Medicine.

(c) Twenty-five lectures or demonstrations in Obstetrics and Gynecology.

(d) Twenty-five lectures or demonstrations in Clinical Microscopy (including Urine Analysis, Blood examinations, etc.) and Autopsy work.

(e) One month in practical dispensing.

(f) Twenty-five lectures or demonstrations in Ophthalmology, Otology and Rhinology and Laryngology.

(g) Ten practical demonstrations in the administration of anesthetics.

(h) Attendance on ten cases of Midwifery.

5. Course prescribed for Homeopathic students:

Candidates wishing to be registered as Homeopathists must conform with the requirements regarding matriculation as found in Section 1.

Such candidates must also have complied with the full curriculum of studies prescribed from time to time by the Council for all medical students, but the full time of attendance upon lectures and hospitals required by the curriculum of the Council may be spent in such Homeopathic Medical Colleges in the United States or Europe as may be recognized by a majority of the Homeopathic members of the Council, and when such teaching body has been established in Ontario, it shall be optional for such candidates to pursue in part or in full the required curriculum in Ontario.

6. Graduates in medicine from recognized colleges outside the Dominion of Canada who desire to qualify themselves for registration must conform to the matriculation required by the Council; and must attend one or more full winter course of lectures in one of the regular medical schools in Ontario, and must complete fully the practical and clinical curriculum required by the Council, and shall pass before the examiners appointed by the Council all the examinations hereinafter prescribed.

Registration of British Medical Practitioners.

Registration in the Register of The College of Physicians and Surgeons of Ontario confers the right to practice medicine, surgery and midwifery in the Province of Ontario under the provisions of The Ontario Medical Act.

It is necessary, according to the provisions of The Ontario Medical Act and Regulations of the Council of The College of Physicians and Surgeons of Ontario, passed in accordance therewith, that any person applying to be registered as a British Medical Practitioner should produce to the Registrar documents or certificates as follows:

1. A Certificate that the applicant is duly registered in the Medical Register of the United Kingdom of Great Britain and Ireland. (This Certificate is obtained from the Registrar of the British Medical Council.)

2.* Satisfactory evidence of identity.

3.* Satisfactory evidence of good character.

4.* Satisfactory evidence that the diploma or diplomas in respect of which the applicant was registered in the Medical Register of the United Kingdom was or were granted to him at a time when he was not domiciled in the Province of Ontario or in the course of a period of not less than five years during the whole of which he resided out of the Province of Ontario.

5. The documents and the prescribed fee (One hundred dollars) should, together with the enclosed forms duly filled in, be transmitted to the address set forth hereunder:

The Registrar of The College of Physicians
and Surgeons of Ontario,
170 University Avenue,
Toronto.

*Blank forms, to be filled in, when satisfying these requirements, may be had upon application to the Registrar of either the British or the Ontario Medical Council.

SECTION III.

Examinations—Date and place, and requirements of.

1. There shall be one Examination held by the Medical Council, and that at the end of the fifth year.

2. Every applicant for this examination must be a graduate of an approved Medical College, and must present certificates of attendance covering a period of five years, except as provided in paragraph 2, section II.

3. The following shall be the subjects for said examination:
(1) Medicine.
(2) Surgery.
(3) Midwifery and Diseases of Women.

4. The examination shall consist of two examinations on each subject: (1) "written" and (2) "oral" and "clinical."

5. Sixty per cent. of the marks will be required to pass in each subject. A candidate must take all three subjects at one examination, but he will only be required to pass subsequently on any subject or subjects upon which he has failed.

6. The examinations shall be held at Toronto, Kingston and London, annually, at such time as shall be fixed by the Annual By-law. There shall also be a Fall Examination at the City of Toronto, beginning the first Tuesday in November of each year, for candidates who have failed in one or more subjects at the Annual Examination.

7. Candidates who intend to be examined by the Homeopathic Examiners shall signify their intention to the Registrar at least two weeks previous to the announcement of the examinations, due notice of which must be given to examiner by Registrar. Homeopathic students are to be examined by examiners approved by a majority of the Homeopathic members of the Council.

8. The Fall Examination for 1915 begins on Tuesday, Nov. 2nd, 1915. The Spring Examination for 1916 begins on Tuesday, May 16th, 1916.

SECTION IV.

Examinations—Duties of Registrar and Board of Examiners.

Rules for the guidance of the Registrar and the Board of Examiners:

1. The Registrar or a Deputy Registrar must be present at every examination, and each student must produce evidence satisfactory to the Registrar or Deputy Registrar of his identity.

2. At the end of each written examination upon any subject, the answers to the questions are to be handed by the candidates to the Registrar, who will open the envelopes, in which they are hereinafter directed to be enclosed, and to each set of papers affix a number by which the author will be known to the Examiners during the examination. The Registrar will then deliver the papers to those members of the Board of Examiners appointed by the Council to examine upon the subject, upon which these candidates have just been writing.

3. The papers when delivered to the members of the Board of Examiners appointed by the Council to examine on the subject, are to be by them examined, and the relative value of answers marked by means of numbers on a blank form which will be furnished to them by the Registrar.

4. The percentage in all subjects of the Professional Examinations shall range from 0 to 100, of which 60 per cent. will be required to pass in each subject.

5. The value awarded by the Examiners to the answers of candidates and confirmed by the Board of Examiners is not to be subject to revision, except by the Council, which may have the papers re-read and revised in special cases of alleged hardship.

6. In the event of any alterations or erasures in the marks of a paper, or of any question in a paper, the same should be initialed by both Examiners.

7. The Examiners shall, on the completion of their work, conjointly certify to the schedule of marks and books. Their report, including schedule of marks and books, completed and duly certified, shall be final, and shall forthwith be filed with the Registrar.

8. The Examiner shall return the schedule to the Registrar, with values inserted, within fifteen days of the close of examinations on his subject. From these values a general schedule shall be prepared by a chartered accountant associated with the Registrar, which schedule shall be inspected and signed by the President before the results are announced.

9. The Registrar, in notifying the members of the Board of Examiners, will direct attention to the following instructions, a copy of which he shall enclose.

(a) In preparation of questions Examiners will confine themselves to the principles common to the standard text-books.

(b) In referring to diseases or operations of any kind, the name of such disease or operation most commonly in use must be employed, and the Examiners shall refrain as far as possible from the use of proper names and ambiguous questions.

(c) In the preparation of the paper, that opposite each question should be placed the value of a full and correct answer thereof—the whole of such numbers to amount to 100.

(d) In the reading of papers the Examiners shall mark in colored pencil what they regard as the numerical value of the answers given for each question opposite the same.

(e) The oral and clinical examinations are to be made as practical, demonstrative or clinical as possible, and shall at least occupy thirty minutes.

(f) Candidates shall be known to the Examiners by numbers only.

(g) There shall be two Examiners in each subject who shall conjointly set and examine each paper and conjointly examine the student in the "Oral and Clinical" Examination.

(h) In the event of any alteration or erasures in the marks of a paper, or of any question in a paper, the same should be initialed by both Examiners.

(i) The Examiners shall meet at the close of the examination for consultation and consideration of reports before these are forwarded to the Registrar. The Examiners shall, on the completion of their work, conjointly certify to the schedules of marks and books. Their report, including schedules of marks and books completed and duly certified shall be final, and shall forthwith be filed with the Registrar.

10. Candidates for oral examinations will be divided into classes alphabetically, and notified of the time at which they shall present themselves for examination. Such students shall wait in an adjoining room, and appear before the Examiners when summoned.

11. The Examiners in each subject shall meet at a convenient point to prepare the examination papers, and shall send each paper to the Registrar by registered mail at least two weeks before the date of examination. (The Examiners shall approve of proofs before printing).

SECTION V.

Examinations—Rules for Candidates in the Examination Hall.

1. Each candidate shall receive from the Registrar a programme containing a list of subjects upon which the candidate

is to be examined, and it will admit him to the examination hall during the progress of the examination upon such subjects, but at no other time.

2. Candidates must write the answers to the questions given by the Examiners legibly and neatly upon one side of each page of a book, which will be furnished to each candidate, and the number of each question, as it appears in the examination paper, is to be put at the head of the answer to it, in such a manner as to have the first page facing outward to the view; the papers then to be folded once and enclosed in an envelope, on the outside of which each candidate is to write his name. The packet is then to be handed to the Registrar or his deputy. No signature, number or sign, by which the writer could be recognized by the Examiner, is to be written or marked on any portion of the book to be enclosed in the envelope.

3. The questions of the Examiners in the Homeopathic subjects will be handed, at the beginning of the general examination on the same subject, by the Registrar or deputy, to such candidates as shall have given him notice in accordance with Section III., sub. sec. 7.

They shall write the answers to these questions in the same hall with the other candidates, and hand their papers, when finished, to the Registrar in the same manner as provided for other candidates, to be by him given for examination to the Homeopathic members of the Board of Examiners appointed to examine on that subject.

4. No candidate will be allowed to leave the hall after the questions are given out, until his answers have been handed in.

5. No one shall be allowed in the hall during the hours of examination, except those who are actually undergoing examination, or members of the Council or officials connected therewith.

6. Any candidate who may have brought any book or reference paper into the hall must deposit it with the Registrar before the examination begins.

7. Candidates must not communicate with each other while examinations are going on, by writing, signs, words, or in any manner whatever.

8. Candidates must at all times bear themselves toward the Registrar or Deputy and Examiners with the utmost deference and respect; and they will not be permitted in any manner to manifest approbation or disapprobation of any member of the Board of Examiners during the progress of the examination.

9. Candidates must not only conduct themselves with decorum while an examination is going on, but they will be held

strictly responsible for any impropriety of conduct during the whole progress both of the written and the oral examinations.

10. Any infraction of the above rules will lead to the ex-elusion of the candidate who is guilty of it, from the remainder of the examination; and he will not receive credit for any examination papers which may have been handed to the Registrar or Deputy previous to his being detected in such misconduct.

11. And he may be debarred from further privileges, at the discretion of the Council.

SECTION VI.

Fees.

1. The following scale of fees has been established by the Council of the College of Physicians and Surgeons of Ontario:

(a) Registration of matriculation $25 00

(b) The Medical Council examination fee, including registration of license 75 00

(This is not to affect any student who is registered prior to 1st of July, 1889).

(c) Registration of additional degrees or titles..... $2 00

(This fee is payable only when the additional titles are registered at different times, but any number of such titles as are allowed to be registered may be put on record at the time of the first registration, without fee).

(d) Diploma of membership of the College $5 00

(This diploma is granted free of charge to all those members of the College who attain their membership by passing the examinations of the College. All other members may obtain it upon application to the Registrar and payment of the above-named fee).

(e) Annual Assessment Dues $2 00

(The payment of this fee, which is imposed annually upon every member of the College, under by-law of the Council, is a sine qua non of good standing in the College. No member of the College can claim recognition as such, before the Courts of Law of the Province of Ontario, to whom the Annual Certificate, representing the payment of this fee, has not been issued).

(f) Fee payable by matriculates of the College, who ask for official certificates of the College, to enable them to appear before the Dominion Medical Council for examination $25 00

(g) Fee payable by licentiates of the College, for
Official Certificate, indicating the date of their registration with the College, and of their being in
good standing in the College, at the time of the
issuing of the Certificate, for presentation to the
Dominion Medical Council. (This applies equally
to those licentiates, who propose offering themselves for examination before the Dominion Medical Council, and those licentiates of not less than
ten years' standing, who seek registration with
the Dominion Medical Council, without Examination) 5 00

(h) Fee payable by licentiates of the Dominion
Medical Council, who ask to be registered as
licentiates of the College of Physicians and Surgeons of Ontario 100 00

(i) Fee payable by licentiates of the Médical Council of Great Britain, who ask to be registered as
licentiates of the College of Physicians and Surgeons of Ontario 100 00

2. All fees must be paid in lawful money of Canada, to the
Treasurer of the College. The Office of the College is at 170
University Avenue, Toronto. Payments may be made in person
or by mail. Payment of Examination fees, when made in person
at the College Office, will be accepted up to two o'clock in the
afternoon, (on Saturdays, up to eleven o'clock in the forenoon).

3. Examination fees to accompany application form of
candidates for Examination, and to be in the hands of the
Registrar not less than two weeks before the date set for the
beginning of the Examinations.

4. No candidate will be admitted to any examination until
the fee for such examination is paid in full.

5. Candidates who have failed in any professional examination in one or more subjects will be allowed to take the next
ensuing Spring examination, without payment of further fee,
but if such examination take place in the Fall the payment of a
fee of twenty-five dollars ($25.00) shall be required for same.

6. A fee of five dollars must accompany all appeals for
reconsideration of examination papers. This fee of five dollars
will be refunded to those candidates only, whose appeals are
granted. (Such appeals for reconsideration of examination
papers will not be entertained, unless made anterior to the date
of the next ensuing meeting of the Council).

Examination Questions, 1914

FINAL EXAMINATION, NOVEMBER, 1914

MEDICINE.

N.B.—Answer five questions only. All questions of equal value.

1. (a) Give the clinical varieties, symptoms and differential diagnosis of smallpox.

(b) Outline the necessary prophylactic measures in connection with a case.

2. (a) Describe the usual development, symptoms and physical signs of acute broncho-penumonia in a child of eighteen months.

(b) Discuss etiology, prognosis, and give your management of a case.

3. (a) Give causation, course, symptoms, and diagnosis of Tabes dorsalis (Locomotor ataxia).

(b) Outline a course of treatment for an early case.

4. Give physical signs, symptoms, course, and differential diagnosis of carcinoma of stomach developing at pyloric orifice.

5. (a) Describe the pathology of arthritis deformans developing in middle-aged subjects.

(b) Discuss its etiology, and give differential diagnosis, course and treatment.

6. Discuss the etiology, pathology, symptoms, physical signs and treatment of an aneurysm of anterior portion of transverse arch of aorta in a man of 42 years.

A. S. LOCKHART,
W. T. CONNELL,
Examiners.

SURGERY.

(1) Answer five questions only.

(2) All questions of equal value (20 marks).

(3) Time 2½ hours.

I. A man with an impassable stricture of Urethra suddenly finds he has retention of urine. Give (a) immediate treatment of the retention. (b) Treatment directed to the restoration of the function of the Urethra.

II. What structures are implicated in fracture of the lower end of the radius (Colles)? (b) Describe the deformity. (c) Outline appropriate treatment.

III. What conditions produce hemorrhage from the Gastro Intestinal tract? (b) Give differential diagnosis between any two. (c) Give treatment of any one.

IV. Give (a) Causes, (b) Symptoms, and (c) treatment of Pyelitis.

V. Give causes of enlargement of Lymphatic Glands of the neck. (b) In what conditions would you remove the glands? (c) Describe the operation.

VI. Give symptoms of fracture of the base of the skull. (b) Outline treatment.

E. SEABORN,
P. STUART,
Examiners.

OBSTETRICS AND GYNAECOLOGY.

Values.

20   1. Anaesthesia in Labour. At what stage is it usually employed, and to what degree is it carried in normal labour? What guides you in the choice of an anaesthetic? Describe your method of administration with a nurse as your only assistant. Mention one complication in the first and one in the second stage of labour where anaesthesia may be necessary.

20   2. Pernicious Vomiting of Pregnancy. When does it usually occur? What are the causes? Describe the clinical course and the results of laboratory investigations in a case going on to a fatal termination. Describe the treatment you would adopt at each stage of the disease.

20   3. How do you calculate the probable date of labour and what are the fallacies? A primiparous patient has gone two weeks past the calculated date of labour. What examination would you make and what findings would determine you to induce labour? Describe the method of induction you would employ.

20   4. Retroflexion of the Uterus. Name the causes. What symptoms may the patient complain of? Describe systematically the physical signs you would find on examination. What conditions would lead you to recommend operative treatment? Decribe the operation you would perform in a married woman 30 years of age.

20   5. A young woman who has had a child three months ago complains of pain in the left side of the abdomen, backache, bearing-down pain and dyspareunia. Discuss the probable diagnosis and indicate the treatment.

R. H. Arthur, M.D.,
B. P. Watson, M.D.,
Examiners.

THEORY AND PRACTICE OF MEDICINE; HOMEOPATHIC.

All questions are of equal value.

1. Give causes and symptoms of acute endocarditis.

2. Give symptoms and pathology in acute pleurisy.

3. How would you treat a case of acute lobar pneumonia?

4. Differentiate symptomatically asthma from oedema of glottis.

5. Differentiate a syphilitic from a tubercular ulcer of pharynx.

6. Give pathological anatomy in acute parenchymatous nephritis.

7. Differentiate erysipelas from erythema.

8. Describe Bell's paralysis; Cheyne-Stokes respiration.

9. What are the early manifestations of pulmonary tuberculosis?

10. Give symptoms of tuberculous meningitis.

W. A. McFall, M.B.,
George L. Husband, M.D.,
Examiners.

SURGERY, HOMEOPATHIC.

All questions are of equal value.

1. Enumerate the recognized degree of burns and describe treatment of each.

2. Describe the objective and subjective symptoms of strangulated hernia, and describe an operation for relief of same.

3. Give causes, diagnosis and treatment of transverse fracture of patella.

4. Describe symptoms of the several stages of hip joint disease. Give the cause.

5. Give minute description for the proper administration of ether for general anaesthesia.

W. A. McFALL, M.B.,
GEORGE L. HUSBAND, M.D.,
Examiners.

MIDWIFERY AND DISEASES OF WOMEN, HOMEOPATHIC.

All questions are of equal value.

1. Name and give measurements of (1) female pelvis, (2) foetal head.

2. Give in detail technique of repairing laceration of perineum, involving floor of vagina.

3. Name the important forms of hemorrhage met with in obstetrical practice, giving causes and treatment of each.

4. How would you treat mastitis; puerperal eclampsia?

5. How would you prepare your patient for delivery and yourself for attendance in a case of labour? Mention armentarium.

W. A. McFALL, M.B.,
GEORGE L. HUSBAND, M.D.,
Examiners.

FINAL EXAMINATIONS, MAY, 1915

MEDICINE.

N.B.—All questions of equal value. Answer 5 questions only.

1. Describe modes of onset, main clinical types, symptoms, differential diagnosis and treatment of epidemic cerebro-spinal meningitis.

2. (a) Give the cause, symptoms, differential diagnosis and treatment of acute rheumatic fever.

(b) Discuss the cardiac complications which may attend it and give physical signs and symptoms by which you would recognize their development.

3. (a) What symptoms would lead you to suspect a case to be one of membranous croup and how would you verify your diagnosis?

(b) Describe in detail your treatment of a case in a child of five years.

4. Discuss the causes, symptoms, and give differential diagnosis of duodenal ulcer.

Briefly outline treatment of a suspected case.

5. (a) Discuss the etiology of acute nephritis.

(b) Describe the symptoms, diagnosis, prognosis and treat_ ment of a case following diphtheria.

6. (a) Give distinguishing characters of psoriasis. Discuss its diagnosis and treatment.

(b) What parts are usually attacked in acne vulgaris? How would you recognize and treat this affection?

A. S. LOCKHART,
WM. GIBSON,
Examiners.

SURGERY.

I. Answer five questions only.

II. Time 2½ hours.

Values.

20   I. A man receives a stab wound in the lower part of the Epigastric region. (a) What symptoms may he present? (b) When would you operate? (c) What structures may be injured? (d) Outline treatment when a hollow viscus has been perforated.

20   II. Describe (a) The anatomical location of an acute Ischio-rectal abscess. (b) Give causes. (c) Symptoms. (d) Treatment and (e) Sequelae.

20   III. Describe (a) A Compound Fracture. (b) Give treatment in detail for such a fracture in the lower Third of Femur. (c) Under what conditions would you plate a fracture?

20   IV. Give the differential diagnosis between dislocation at the hip, and fracture of the neck of the Femur.

20   V. Give (a) Etiology, (b) Symptoms, (c) Treatment of Tetanus.

20   -   VI. Describe the symptoms produced when the Musculo-Spiral Nerve has been implicated in a fracture, (b) Give treatment.

E. Seaborn,
P. Stuart,
Examiners.

OBSTETRICS AND GYNAECOLOGY.

Values.

20   1. Pyelitis Complicating Pregnancy. Give symptoms, diagnosis and treatment.

20   2. A patient fifty years of age, three years past the menopause, consults you regarding a slight irregular bloody discharge. Discuss the means you would take to investigate the case, possible diagnosis and treatment you would advise.

20   3. How would you conduct the first and second stages of a breech delivery?

20   4. Give differential diagnosis between an Uterine Myoma and a Pregnancy at the fourth month.

20   5. A young woman becomes infected with Gonorrhoea. Discuss the various conditions which may ensue and treatment.

F. A. Cleland,
W. A. Thomson,
Examiners.

MEDICINE, HOMEOPATHIC.

All questions are of equal value.

1. Give etiology, symptoms and treatment of Cerebro-spinal Meningitis.

2. Describe accurately, the eruption of Measles, Scarlet Fever, and Varicella.

3. Differentiate between Pericarditis with effusion and dilatation of heart.

4. Give causes, symptoms and treatment of Haemophilia.

5. Differentiate between Croupous or Lobar Pneumonia and Catarrhal or Lobular Pneumonia.

6. Give etiology, characteristic symptoms, and treatment of Acute Chorea.

7. What is Herpes Zoster? Give causes and treatment.

8. What are the causes and treatment of palpitation of heart.

9. Differentiate between Diphtheria and Follicular Tonsillitis.

10. What are the possible complications in the third week of typhoid fever? Give signs, symptoms and treatment of each.

W. A. McFall, M.B.,
George L. Husband, M.D.,
Examiners.

SURGERY, HOMEOPATHIC.

All questions of equal value.

1. What is Phlebitis? Give causes, symptoms and treatment.

2. Give etiology, symptoms and treatment of Tetanus.

3. What is Synovitis? Give pathology, symptoms and treatment.

4. Give differential diagnosis between acute inflammation of middle ear and mastoiditis.

5. Give symptoms and treatment of movable kidney.

6. Give evidences and treatment of a wound penetrating the bladder.

7. Give symptoms, diagnosis and treatment of Hydrocele of tunica vaginalis.

8. Give diagnosis, possible complications and treatment of fracture of lower third of femur.

9. Give differential diagnosis of renal colic.

10. Give symptoms of brain tumor.

W. A. McFall, M.B.,
George L. Husband, M.D.,
Examiners.

MEMBERS OF THE COLLEGE OF PHYSICIANS AND SURGEONS OF ONTARIO, WHO HAVE ATTAINED THEIR MEMBERSHIP BY EXAMINATION SINCE THE ISSUE OF THE ONTARIO MEDICAL REGISTER, DECEMBER 31st, 1907.

1911 Adams, Frederick, Coboconk, Ont.
1908 Adams, R. T., Lindsay.
1910 Adams, William F. M., 605 Euclid Avenue, Toronto.
1913 Adams, William MacDonald, 267 Queen St. W., Toronto.
1914 Aiken, Leslie Roy, Courtright, Ont.
1908 Aikenhead, A. E., Brucefield.
1915 Aikenhead, Joseph William, Brucefield, Ont.
1911 Ainley, William Edward, Bridgewater, N.S.
1915 Aitken, George William Alexander, London, Ont., 55 Askin St.
1912 Alexander, Charles Cleland, Seaforth, Ont.
1912 Alexander, John Gordon, Dunnville, Ont.
1913 Alexander, Seeyman Laird, Cavalier, North Dakota, U.S.A.
1910 Allin, Norman G., Bowmanville.
1911 Allison, Duncan, Belgrave, Ont.
1915 Allison, Hubert Charles, London, Ont., 3 Becher St.
1911 Alport, Edward B., Orillia, Ont.
1908 Anderson, C. E., Philadelphia, U.S.A.
1913 Anderson, Frank Cecil, 125 Union St., Kingston, Ont.
1910 Anderson, George W., 5 Castle Frank Ave., Toronto.
1910 Anderson, James Le Roy, Ailsa Craig.
1910 Anderson, William Edmund, Kingston.
1914 Anglin, George Chambers, 21 St. Vincent St., Toronto.
1912 Annett, Ivan Erle, Watford, Ont.
1913 Argue, Henry Harold, Shawville, Que.
1908 Armour, R. G., Toronto.
1911 Arnold, Walter Clifford, Zephyr, Ont.
1912 Arseneau, Joseph Camil Eugene, Robitaille, Bonaventure County, Que.
1910 Atkinson, Charles Francis, Tilsonburg.
1914 Austin, James Priestly, 30 Wyndott St. W., Windsor, Ont.
1915 Avery, William Hambly, Strathroy, Ont.
1912 Axford, Edwin Charles, Talbotville, Ont.
1910 Bailey, George Taylor, Cochrane.
1908 Baillie, W. H., Toronto.
1915 Baker, Daniel MacTavish, Fort William, Ont., 136 North Franklin Street.
1911 Baker, Ernest Symons, 21 Sparkhall Ave., Toronto.

1909   Baker, Herbert Wm., 29 Euclid Ave., Toronto, Ont.
1911   Balfour, Edmund Burke, 333 Queen's Ave., London, Ont.
1911   Ball, Harold De Witt, 178 Sherbourne St., Toronto.
1915   Ball, Roy, Toronto, Ont., 628 Manning Ave.
1914   Ballantyne, Charles Clarke, 262 St. George St., Toronto.
1910   Barclay, Gideon O., Winchester.
1912   Barker, Harold Richmond, Thornbury, Ont.
1910   Barker, Percy Weeks, Stratford.
1911   Barker, Ralph R., Forfar, Ont.
1915   Barrett, Henry Merrett, Salford, Ont.
1912   Barton, Newton James, Beeton, Ont.
1914   Bastedo, Albert Frederick, Bracebridge, Ont.
1912   Bateman, William Russell, Thomasburg, Ont.
1908   Bates, G. A., Toronto.
1909   Bates, Henry Kendall, 15 Barton Ave., Toronto.
1908   Baxter, Alice, Toronto.
1915   Bean, John Arthur, Clinton, Ont.
1914   Beatty, James Campbell, Toronto.
1914   Beaven, John Reginald, Hespeler, Ont.
1910   Belfie, Gerald, Gananoque.
1911   Belfry, Roy Aubrey, 535 King St. East, Toronto.
1913   Bell, Harold, Collingwood, Ont.
1908   Bell, H. W., Port Hope.
1909   Bell, Irving Russell, 72 Robert St., Toronto, Ont.
1914   Bell, William Ker, Meaford, Ont., Box 435.
1908   Bennette, F. R., Palmerston.
1912   Benson, Harry Wordsworth, Ross Mount, Ont.
1908   Bethune, W., Ryckman's Corners.
1908   Bice, J. G., Brinsley.
1911   Biggs, W., Hallville, Ont.
1915   Binkley, George Ernest, Toronto, Hosp. for Sick Children.
1912   Birchard, Cecil Clinton, Coboconk, Ont.
1913   Birks, William Herbert, Dundas, Ont.
1911   Bissell, Edgar Sheuell, Row's Corners, Ont.
1915   Black, Howard, Stroud, Ont.
1908   Black, H. H., London.
1908   Blanchard, E., Leaskdale.
1913   Bodkin, Wilfrid Andrew Thomas, 50 Craig St., London, Ont.
1914   Bond, James Ernest, 262 Broadview Ave., Toronto.
1915   Bond, Roy Armstrong, 18 College St., Toronto, Ont.
1912   Bonner, Frank Aubrey, Bayham, Ont.
1912   Bonsar, William Oscar, 54 Macpherson Ave., Toronto.
1911   Booth, Gordon Elliott, City View, Ottawa, Ont.
1909   Bowden, Herbert McGregor, 336 Alfred St., Kingston.
1912   Bowman, Fred Beninger, Hamilton, Ont.
1908   Boyce, H. A., Murray.
1908   Boyd, E., Toronto.

1910   Boyd, Julian Southworth, Simcoe.
1908   Boyer, G. F., Kincardine.
1912   Bradley, John Courtland, Fenaghvale, Ont.
1915   Brady, Robert Emmet, Lindsay, Ont.
1911   Brandon, Thomas Alexander, Forest, Ont.
1914   Bremner, John Murray, Camilla, Ont.
1914   Brereton, Charles Hulse, 76 Rosemont Ave., Toronto.
1912   Breslin, Louis Judah, 436 Adelaide St. West, Toronto.
1911   Breuls, Robert W., 559 Euclid Ave., Toronto.
1911   Brewster, Francis Arthur, Beeton, Ont.
1909   Bricker, James G., Gorrie, Ont.
1909   Briggs, Byron Edward, Burlington.
1910   Bright, Robert James Rose, Wiarton.
1913   Brisco, Clarence Alfred, Chatham, Ont.
1915   Broad, Charles Oscar, Little Britain, Ont.
1913   Brockenshire, Freeman Albert, Talbotville, Ont.
1908   Broddy, W. A., Uxbridge.
1913   Brodey, Abraham, 324 Palmerston Boul., Toronto.
1909   Bromley, John Edwin, Pembroke, Ont.
1915   Brooke, Rufus John Whitby, Georgetown, Ont.
1910   Brown, Allan Gowans, 62 Madison Ave., Toronto.
1909   Brown, Caroline Sophia, 4 Richmond St. East, Toronto.
1913   Brown, Chester Pettit, Paris, Ont.
1910   Brown, Clarence Egerton, 420 Oxford St., London.
1912   Brown, Hubert Arthur Wood, 166 Madison Ave., Toronto
1914   Brown, Harold Ernest, 474 George St., Peterborough, Ont.
1909   Brown, James B., Paisley, Ont.
1909   Brown, Percy Gordon, 116 Hazelton Ave., Toronto.
1910   Brunet, Ernest, Clarence Creek.
1912   Bryans, Frederick Thomas, Jamestown, Ont.
1908   Bryden, W. H., Brampton.
1911   Buck, Frederick Herbert, Norwood, Ont.
1908   Buck, G. S., Lindsay.
1911   Buck, Harold, Port Rowan, Ont.
1913   Buck, Lloyd Lawrence, Kepler, Ont.
1913   Burgess, John Fred, 467 9th St. E., Owen Sound, Ont.
1911   Burgess, William Arnott, Box 203, Leamington, Ont.
1912   Burke, Frederick Sypher, Fergus, Ont.
1914   Burnham, Howard Hampden, 55 Warren Rd., Toronto.
1909   Burns, Harold Stanley, Jarvis, Ont.
1908   Burns, J., Palmerston.
1912   Butt, William Henry, 222 Ridout St., London, Ont.
1911   Butterwick, George Edward, Aylmer, Ont.
1915   Buttle, Walter William, Cobden, Ont., R.R. No. 5.
1911   Byers, James Campbell, Eganville, Ont.
1911   Byrne, Edward Patrick, 362 Johnson St., Kingston, Ont.
1908   Calder, Margaret C., Innisfail, Ont.
1914   Caldwell, George Leonard, Shanty Bay, Ont.

1911 Caldwell, Robert Atchison, Murillo, Ont.
1908 Callahan, T. H., Wooler.
1912 Cameron, Donald Robert, Lancaster, Ont.
1914 Cameron, Keith Wilson, 28 Elgin Ave., Toronto.
1909 Cameron, W. Elmore, Springvale, Ont.
1909 Campbell, Alexander Douglas, Owen Sound, Ont.
1909 Campbell, Andrew L., Belmont, Ont.
1911 Campbell, Angus Alexander, Shanty Bay, Ont.
1911 Campbell, Duncan Alexander, North Bay, Ont.
1913 Campbell, James A., Belmont, Ont.
1911 Campbell, James Patrick, Arthur, Ont.
1911 Campbell, John, Parry Sound, Ont.
1909 Campbell, John De Lendrecie, Arnprior, Ont.
1911 Campbell, John George Alexander, 76 Evelyn Cres., West
      Toronto.
1908 Campbell, M. B., Toronto.
1911 Campbell, Roscoe, Gravenhurst, Ont.
1915 Campbell, Walter Ruggles, Toronto, 249 Brunswick Ave.
1912 Campbell, William Charles, Belleville, Ont.
1912 Cann, William Richard, Oshawa, Ont.
1908 Cannon, O. A., Walkerton.
1914 Cardwell, William Arthur, 1002 Bloor W., Toronto.
1912 Carleton, George Wylie Dundas, Thornhill, Ont.
1909 Carmichael, Duncan, 39 Union St., Kingston.
1909 Carmichael, Samuel Victor, Spencerville, Ont.
1915 Carpenter, Theodore Augustus, Port Dover, Ont.
1909 Carswell, Duncan F., Elora, Ont.
1914 Cascaden, John Harold, 454 Ontario St., Toronto.
1910 Casselman, Simon Bismark, Williamsburg.
1914 Casserly, Michael Joseph, Hamilton, Mont., U.S.A.
1913 Cathcart, John Philip Selby, Courtright, Ont.
1915 Cathcart, William Allen, Courtright, Ont.
1912 Caven, William Ernest, Erindale, Ont.
1909 Cays, Frederick William, 128 Barrie St., Kingston, Ont.
1911 Chamberlain, Harry William, Aylmer West, Ont.
1909 Chapman, Frederick Robert, Essex, Ont.
1911 Charbonneau, Joseph Edmond, Chelmsford, Ont.
1910 Charlebois, Joseph Albert, Fournier.
1908 Chenworth, Nancy Redger, Michel, B.C.
1910 Childs, James Roy Nelson, 21 Becher St., London.
1908 Christie, J., Webbwood.
1910 Christie, John Duncan, Toronto.
1912 Christie, Neil Alexander, Stayner, Ont.
1912 Clark, Charles William Lloyd, Toronto.
1910 Clark, David Alexander, 452 Euclid Ave., Toronto.
1909 Clark, David Wesley, Ballyduff, Ont.
1914 Clarke, Harold, 41 Olive Ave., Toronto.
1914 Clegg, Frank Robert, 207 Simcoe St., London, Ont.

1914 Clifford, Ernest James, 305 Pape Ave., Toronto.
1912 Coates, Llewellyn Herbert, 133 Brant St., Brantford, Ont.
1908 Cockburn, G. L., Sturgeon Falls.
1912 Cody, Morley Garnet, Newmarket, Ont.
1912 Cody, William Macpherson, 32 Emerald St. S., Hamilton.
1910 Collins, Albert, Niagara Falls.
1912 Collins, James Daniel, London, Ont.
1912 Colvill, Robert, Port Perry, Ont.
1914 Conn, Hartly Robert, Thornbury, Ont.
1910 Conn, Leighton C., St. Catharines.
1914 Connelly, Harold Edward, 577 McLaren St., Ottawa.
1908 Connolly, H. A., Kingston.
1914 Cook, Lorne Hall, 229 Albany Ave., Toronto.
1909 Cooke, Hugh M., 108 Carlton St., Toronto.
1913 Cooke, Kenneth Edgar, Binbrook, Ont.
1911 Copeland, Gordon Grote, 160 Spadina Rd., Toronto.
1908 Cornett, W. F., Kingston.
1915 Cornish, Charles Cecil, Ingersoll, Ont.
1912 Corrigan, Leo Joseph, 156 Wellington St., Kingston, Ont.
1915 Cosbie, Waring Gerald, 30 Douglas Drive, Toronto.
1913 Costain, William Alfred, 21 Egerton St., Brantford, Ont.
1909 Cotnam, Ira D., Pembroke, Ont.
1915 Cotton, James Henry, 703 Spadina Ave., Toronto.
1914 Couillard, Albert Joseph, 35 Lloyd St., Ottawa, Ont.
1911 Coulombe, Paul O., 1295 Bordeaux Street, Montreal, Que.
1909 Coulter, William George G., 68 Victoria Ave., Windsor, Ont.
1915 Coutts, Eldon Douglas, Toronto, 65 Gothic Avenue.
1914 Cowling, Edna May, Toronto.
1910 Craig, Delmar Allan, Kemptville.
1914 Craig, Vernon H., Kingston, Ont., 376 Albert St.
1909 Craise, Oliver B., Petrolea, Ont.
1914 Crane, Richard Edwin, 50 Simpson Ave., Toronto.
1908 Crann, G. R., Queensville.
1909 Crassweller, Henry, Sarnia, Ont.
1911 Crawford, Clarence Moffat, 228 Sydenham St., Kingston.
1913 Crowley, Lawrence Edmond, 110 Ordnance St., Kingston.
1911 Crowe, Henry Stanley, Central Onslow, Colchester Co., N.S.
1910 Cruickshank, William Ewart, Chatham.
1915 Cruickshank, William Douglas, Hamilton, Ont., 219 Main Street, West.
1911 Cruise, William Wilson, Port Dover, Ont.
1910 Culbertson, Norman Edward, Meaford.
1910 Culham, Hubert Anthony, 147 Roxborough St. E., Toronto.
1913 Cumberland, Thomas Daily, Rosemont, Ont.
1910 Cunningham, John Donald, Sarnia.
1915 Cunningham, John Grant, 1024 Heuleaze Avenue, Moose Jaw, Sask.
1912 Cunningham, Stella Alice, 144 Bloor St. West, Toronto.

1910 Curry, Douglas V., 224 Beverley St., Toronto.
1908 Dafoe, A. R., Madoc.
1915 Dale, Gordon McIntyre, 35 Wellington St., St. Thomas.
1909 Davidson, Robert Edward, Beachburg, Ont.
1912 Davies, Andrew Pritchard, Hull, Que.
1910 Davis, Daniel W., Brockville.
1914 Davis, Frederic George, Ivy, Ont.
1911 Davis, Robert Edwin, Ivy, Ont.
1910 Davis, Robert William, Staffa.
1910 Davis, Walter, Onondaga.
1910 Dawson, Lionel Montrose, 149 Patterson Ave., Ottawa.
1914 Day, Oswald John, Orillia, Ont.
1910 Day, William E. C., Shallow Lake.
1911 Defries, Archibald Stuart, 866 Trafalgar St., London, Ont.
1912 Defries, Robert Davies, 223 Westmoreland Ave., Toronto.
1911 Defries, William James, 60 Bismark Ave., Toronto, Ont.
1915 Delahaye, Allan Lester, Pembroke, Ont.
1915 De La Matter, I.
1912 Derby, Leonard Lansdowne, Plantagenet, Ont.
1913 DesRosiers, Arthur, Rockland, Ont.
1914 Detweiler, Herbert Knutsen, R.R. No. 3, Berlin, Ont.
1909 Dewar, Roderick D., Glen Sandfield, Ont.
1911 Dey, William Frederick, Simcoe, Ont.
1911 Dickson, Ivan W., 8 Spadina Road, Toronto.
1912 Digby, Reginald Winniett, 64 Wellington St., Brantford.
1910 Dingwall, Donald Grant, Lancaster.
1908 Dixon, J. A., Almonte.
1914 Dobbie, John Albert, Kingston, Ont., 45 Clergy St.
1911 Doherty, Mary Agatha, Eglinton, Ont.
1908 Donevan, F. J., Gananoque.
1911 Dorsey, Charles Frederick, Collingwood, Ont.
1913 Douglas, Clair Locksley, 7 Isabel St., St. Thomas, Ont.
1914 Douglas, Hamnett Townley, 250 Sherbrooke W., Montreal, Que.
1910 Douglas, Leon Alexander, Yarmouth Centre.
1912 Douglas, Roy Gladstone, Meaford, Ont.
1914 Dover, Harry, 27 York St., Ottawa, Ont.
1909 Downing, John Henry, 408 Burwell St., London, Ont.
1914 Drake, Theodore George Gustavus Harwood, North Bay.
1914 Duck, John Albert, Toronto.
1912 Duff, Thomas Alexander Jamieson, Cookstown, Ont.
1908 Duncan, J., Toronto.
1915 Duncan, John Henderson, Bruce Mines, Ont.
1913 Dunfield, Charles Frances, Petrolia, Ont.
1911 Dunn, James Moses, Elgin, Ont.
1915 Dunning, George Percival, Riceville, Ont.
1914 Dure, Franklin Mortimer, Uxbridge, Ont.
1911 Durocher, Ulysses Joseph, Ojibwa, Ont.

1910   Dwyre, Jamés G., 11 East 18 St., New York City, N.Y.
1911   Eager, Joseph Culloden, Waterdown, Ont.
1912   Eagles, Allan Sloan, Meaford, Ont.
1915   Earl, Allan Boyd, Athens, Ont.
1910   Earle, George N. L., Omemee.
1914   Eberhart, Francis Louis, Seaforth, Ont.
1915   Eby, Wilbert Harold, Cookstown, Ont.
1910   Ecclestone, Wilfred Marlow, 1 Warren Road, Toronto.
1908   Edward, M. L., Petrolia.
1908   Elliott, B. S., Ingersoll.
1912   Elliott, Edwin, Chesaning, Mich., U.S.A.
1911   Ellis, Stayner, Windsor, Ont.
1910   Emerson, Harry G., Wheatley.
1909   Emmett, Harry Lloyd, Fonthill, Ont.
1911   Etherington, Frederick, 218 Albert St., Kingston, Ont.
1912   Evans, Donald Thomas, Port Perry, Ont.
1912   Evans, Edgar George, Virginia, Ont.
1908   Evans, J. A., Islington.
1911   Eyres, Herbert Henry, Lindsay, Ont.
1909   Fader, William Richard, 17 London St., Windsor, Ont.
1914   Faed, Percival Elmore, Woodville, Ont.
1908   Falkner, A. E., Williamstown.
1911   Faris, Matthew Norman, Bradford, Ont.
1908   Fauld, R. W., Burwell Road.
1915   Fauman, David Haymes, 83 Kelly St., Rochester, N.Y.
1911   Fee, Donald Lewis, Camden East, Ont.
1909   Feldhans, Henry William, Copper Cliff, Ont.
1909   Ferguson, Alexander, Heaslip, New Ontario.
1914   Ferguson, Hugh Edgar, Toronto, 371 Spadina Rd.
1909   Ferguson, Horace James, London, Ont.
1911   Ferguson, Rosslyn Montague, Smith's Falls, Ont.
1913   Ferguson, William David, 35 Hess St. S., Hamilton, Ont.
1911   Ferguson, W. Ewart, 264 College St., Toronto.
1912   Ferrier, David Joseph Norman, Belwood, Ont.
1915   Ferrier, Gordon, Mimico, Ont.
1910   Fettes, James M., Le Mars, Iowa.
1909   Fielding, Wm. M., 539 Brunswick Ave., Toronto.
1910   Fisher, Stuart M., London.
1908   Fleming, A. G., Toronto.
1913   Fletcher, Andrew Alyon, 532 Huron St., Toronto.
1914   Flock, George Murray, Burlington, Ont.
1913   Flood, Anthony, James, Box 745, Sault Ste. Marie, Ont.
1909   Folinsbee, Francis J., 2 Bellwoods Park, Toronto.
1911   Foster, Gerald J., 255 Macpherson Ave., Toronto.
1912   Fotheringham, Susie L., Toronto.
1914   Foulds, Gordon Sutcliffe, 58 Triller Ave., Toronto.
1909   Fowler, Jordan M., Petrolea, Ont.
1911   Francis, Robert B., Ingersoll, Ont.

1910 Fraser, Maxwell John, 2 Douro St., Stratford.
1915 Fraser, Robert Howard, Chatham, Ont., R.R. No. 3.
1911 Fraser, Wilburt Grieve, Pembroke, Ont.
1915 Freeman, William Paul, Lucknow, Ont.
1910 Fripp, George Downing, 350½ Somerset St., Ottawa.
1913 Frost, Robert Oakley, Kinmount, Ont.
1912 Fuller, Charles Leroy Russell, Ruthven, Ont.
1915 Furlong, Harry Garrett, Norwich, Ont.
1914 Gaboury, William Lawrence, Lefaivre, Ont.
1909 Gaby, Robert Edward, 44 Beaconsfield Ave., Toronto.
1912 Galbraith, Douglas James, Dutton, Ont.
1910 Galbraith, Thomas M., Thornbury.
1912 Gardiner, John Alexander, Walton, Ont.
1911 Gardiner, John Nelles McKim, Westmeath, Ont.
1914 Gardiner, William John, Mount Forest, Ont.
1911 Gardner, Percy Newby, 28 Lake Front, Kew Beach. Tor.
1910 Gallie, John Gordon, Barrie.
1909 Gandier, Joseph C., Newburgh, Ont.
1911 Geiger, William, Hensall, Ont.
1912 George, Herbert Clegg, Port Hope, Ont.
1910 George, Nelson, 262 Ottaway Ave., London.
1910 Gibson, James Robert, Millbank.
1911 Gillam, George J., Woodstock, Ont.
1911 Gillespie, Andrew Taylor, Box 102 Galt, Ont.
1910 Gillespie, William, Seaforth.
1911 Gillie, James Christopher, Chapleau, Ont.
1911 Gilmour, William Norman, 4 Clarissa, Brockville, Ont.
1908 Glanfield, W. J., Jarvis.
1915 Glenn, Leonard Albert, Adelaide, Ont.
1914 Gliddon, George Clarence, Union, Ont.
1913 Gliddon, Rupert William, Union, Ont.
1912 Gliddon, William Osborne, 24 Regent St., Ottawa.
1911 Glionna, George Anthony Joseph, 207 Beverley St., Toronto.
1913 Glover, Thomas Joseph, 33 Bolton Ave., Toronto, Ont.
1915 Gordon, Edith Hamilton, Toronto, 467 Spadina Ave.
1912 Gordon, Howard Hilman, Manotick, Ont.
1912 Graham, Charles Robert, Arnprior, Ont.
1911 Graham, Clarence Wentworth, Goderich, Ont.
1913 Graham, Grattan Clifford, Fenelon Falls, Ont.
1910 Graham, James Lorne, 167 Mutchmore St., Ottawa.
1915 Graham, Philip Victor, Uxbridge, Ont.
1914 Graham, Malcolm David, Arnprior, Ont.
1911 Graham, Roscoe Reid, Lobo, Ont.
1915 Graham, Thomas Fleck, Brantford, Ont.
1908 Gray, G. C., Wabuno.
1910 Greenlees, John Carey, 103 Elgin Ave., Ottawa.
1913 Greer, George Garnet, 356 Aylmer St., Peterboro, Ont.
1911 Guest, Edna Mary, 700 Bathurst St., Toronto.

1915 Guest, Freeman Reginald, R.R. No. 5, London, Ont.
1915 Guilfoyle, Thomas Reginald, 94 Stanley St., London, Ont.
1915 Guy, Dan Henry, Maxwell P.O., Ont.
1914 Guyatt, Benjamin Leslie, Binbrook, Ont.
1912 Guyatt, Richard Emerson, Binbrook, Ont.
1911 Hackett, Walter Lett, Belfast, Ont.
1910 Haffey, Matthew Joseph, 216 Wilton Ave., Toronto.
1912 Hagmeier, John Edwin, Hespeler, Ont.
1912 Hagmeier, Louis Gordon, Hespeler, Ont.
1910 Hale, George Carleton, 718 Waterloo St., London.
1911 Hale, William, Jr., Gananoque, Ont.
1912 Hall, Hector Clayton, Fort Qu'Appelle, Sask.
1910 Hall, Morton Eldred, Gore Bay.
1913 Halliday, Armond Allan, Chesley, Ont.
1911 Hambly, William Rellison, Napanee, Ont.
1911 Hamilton, C. Dickinson, Cornwall, Ont.
1911 Hamilton, George Harold Ross, Guelph, Ont.
1909 Hamilton, Laura S., 62 Clarence Ave., Toronto.
1909 Hamilton, Robt. Joseph, Collingwood, Ont.
1914 Hamilton, William, 31 Summerhill Ave., Toronto.
1914 Hamilton, William Gordon, Elgin, Ont.
1912 Hand, William Thomas, Byng Inlet, Ont.
1915 Haney, William Carroll, 638 Euclid Ave., Toronto, Ont.
1915 Hanley, James Bernard, Midland, Ont.
1911 Hanley, Thomas Richard, Midland, Ont.
1911 Hanna, Gordon McClelland, 94 Wellington St., Brantford.
1914 Hannah, Beverley, 15 South Drive, Toronto, Ont.
1912 Harcourt, William Vernon, Arthur, Ont.
1909 Harkness, James Graham, Irena P.O., Ont.
1911 Harper, Frederick Samuel, 33 Tisdale St., Hamilton, Ont.
1915 Harris, Charles Augustus, Lakeside, Ont.
1908 Harrison, F. C., 29 Roxborough St. West, Toronto.
1911 Harrison, Howard D., 32 Borden St., Toronto, Ont.
1909 Harrison, John P., Dunnville, Ont.
1912 Hart, Alfred Purvis, Wilfrid, Ont.
1908 Hartman, C. C., Aurora.
1914 Hartry, Russell E., Seaforth, Ont.
1911 Harvey, Francis Rudd, Plenty, Sask.
1910 Harvie, Charles A., Orillia, Ont.
1912 Harvie, Horace Hanly, Coldwater, Ont.
1909 Harvie, William Arthur, Orillia, Ont.
1912 Hassard, Frank Russell, Toronto.
1913 Hastings, Elgin Rowland, Stouffville, Ont.
1912 Hayes, Ethel Millicent, 224 Davenport Rd., Toronto.
1914 Hayes, Ivan Dwight, 224 Davenport Rd., Toronto.
1915 Hayes, Joseph Wilbert, 219 Park St., Peterboro, Ont.
1910 Haywood, Alfred Kimball, 529 Sherbourne St., Toronto.
1908 Hazelwood, J. F., West Toronto.

1910   Healey, James Joseph, 37 Prince Arthur Ave., Toronto.
1915   Hearn, Percival, 1369 Queen St. W., Toronto.
1914   Heffering, Harold, 450 Sherbourne St., Toronto.
1912   Henders, Clarence Wellesley, Port Perry, Ont.
1910   Henderson, Edward Kennedy, 34 Brunswick Ave., Toronto.
1914   Hewitt, Samuel Ross DeLap, 1049 Bathurst St., Toronto.
1909   Hewlett, George Patrick, Ottawa, Ont.
1909   Heyd, Charles Gordon, 418 Sherbourne St., Toronto.
1913   Hicks, William Joseph, Kars, Ont.
1909   Hill, Clarence Edgar, 53 Brunswick Ave., Toronto.
1913   Hodgins, George Lyall, Lucan, Ont.
1908   Hodgson, E. G., Toronto.
1915   Hollis, Karl ⁻ ˈ⁻⁓ᵊrd, Hamilton, Bermuda.
1909   Holme, Herbert Richard, Oil Springs, Ont.
1908   Holmes, R. E., London.
1911   Holmes, Shirley Morell, Chatham, Ont.
1913   Home, Robert 674 Spadina Ave., Toronto, Ont.
1910   Hopkins, Bruce Holmes, Lindsay, Ont.
1911   Hopper, David Alexander, 255 Brunswick Ave., Toronto.
1914   Horkins, Richard Earl, 160 Bleecker St., Toronto.
1909   Horton, Bertrand Blake, Napanee, Ont.
1911   Horton, Elijah Maitland, Roblin, Ont.
1912   Howard, Clarence Almoner, Athens, Ont.
1914   Hubbell, Earl Darius, Thamesville, Ont.
1908   Huehnergard, H., Berlin.
1914   Humphrey, John Nelson, Tara, Ont.
1908   Hunter, A. W., Durham.
1911   Huntsman, A. G., 239 Fern Ave., Toronto.
1914   Hurley, John Joseph, 6 Dundonald St., Toronto.
1909   Hurst, Reuben L., Freeborn, Ont.
1909   Hurtubise, Joseph Ravel, Verner, Ont.
1910   Husband, George Lionel, 129 Main St. West, Hamilton.
1912   Hutchinson, Fred, Sarnia, Ont.
1910   Hutchinson, William G., Port Rowan, Ont.
1910   Hutton, James Borthwick, 288 Earle St., Kingston.
1910   Hutton, Thomas O., Berlin, Ont.
1911   Huxtable, Edward Walton, Sunderland, Ont.
1911   Huyck, Philip Hyatt, 245 Brock St., Kingston, Ont.
1910   Hyland, Gordon, 296 St. George St., Toronto.
1911   Imrie, Cyril Gray, Whitehall, Mich.
1913   Ireland, Richard Alfred, Trenton, Ont.
1913   Irwin, David Campbell, 8 Ossington Ave., Ottawa, Ont.
1911   Jackes, Hervey Lee, 1315 Yonge Street, Toronto.
1910   Jackson, Gordon Park, 208 Cowan Ave., Toronto.
1911   James, Arthur Brown, Brantford, Ont.
1910   James, Harry J., Linden, Wis.
1908   Jamieson, C. V., Guelph.
1911   Jamieson, David Bradshaw, Durham, Ont.

1910   Jamieson, Dougald, Glenarm, Ont.
1910   Jamieson, Leonard Foster, Birmingham, Mich.
1911   Jamieson, Ross Alexander, Mount Forest, Ont.
1910   Jamieson, William, Wellandport.
1914   Jeffs, Howard Brown, 2491 Yonge St., Toronto.
1911   Jepson, Gordon Leigh, 240 Pall Mall St., London, Ont.
1911   Johnson, Herbert Edgar, Randolph, Ont.
1909   Johnston, Arthur Clifford, 49 York St., Kingston.
1908   Johnston, H. B., Vermillion.
1908   Johnston, H. W., Midland.
1910   Johnston, John A., Strongville, Ont.
1911   Johnston, Robert Edmund, 589 Bathurst St., Toronto.
1909   Johnston, Thomas James, Carthage, Ont.
1908   Jones, A. E., Toronto.
1911   Jones, Herbert, Toronto.
1912   Jones, Lloyd Arnold, Glanford, Ont.
1914   Jones, Samuel Orville Hughes, R.R. No. 7, London, Ont.
1915   Jones, William Alfred, R.R. No. 8, London, Ont.
1910   Jordan, Dennis J., 116 Barrie St., Kingston.
1915   Joyce, Harry Gordon, Bronte, Ont.
1911   Jupp, Jim Broadfoot, 322 Wilton Ave., Toronto, Ont.
1909   Kauffman, Victor S., 70 Winchester St., Toronto.
1911   Kay, Alexander Douglas Wallace, 35 Cameron Ave., Windsor, Ont.
1909   Kearns, David Austin, 150 Wilfred St., Ottawa, Ont.
1911   Kearns, Joseph Aloysius, Barrie, Ont.
1912   Keeley, Joseph Austin, Arthur, Ont.
1913   Keillor, Benjamin Franklin, Wallacetown, Ont.
1911   Kelly, Anthony John, Railton, Ont.
1911   Kelly, B. E., Bridgenorth, Ont.
1910   Kelly, Charles B., Guelph, Ont.
1911   Kelly, F. J., Railton, Ont.
1909   Kelly, Joseph M., Addison, Ont.
1915   Kelly, Thomas Francis, Orillia, Ont.
1911   Kendrick, George Bryce, Comber, Ont.
1912   Kennedy, William Andrew, Kingston, Ont.
1908   Kenny, R. Y., Sarnia.
1909   Keyes, John Elwood, Oakwood, Ont.
1910   Kidd, George Claude, Trenton, Ont.
1910   Kidd, George Edward, Prospect, Ont.
1910   Kidd, John Edward, Mitchell.
1911   King, Perry Orr, St. Thomas, Ont.
1912   Kinsella, Malcolm Daniel Boyd, North Bay, Ont.
1910   Kinsey, Albert L., Bracebridge, Ont.
1915   Kinsey, Harold Ivan, Chatham, Ont.
1908   Kirby, P. J., Arthur.
1911   Kirby, Thomas Sylvester, Arthur, Ont.
1912   Kirby, Walter James, Toronto.

1914	Kister, Charles Otto Earle, Chippewa, Ont.
1911	Kitt, Allan Norman, Lucan, Ont.
1913	Knight, Charles Fraser, Moosejaw, Sask.
1914	Knox, James Edward, 18 Elm Grove, Toronto.
1915	Koljonen, Heikki, 124 Machar Ave., Port Arthur, Ont.
1909	Krupp, Weston, New Dundee, Ont.
1908	Lackner, H. M., Berlin.
1914	Laframboise, Jean Marie, St. Eugene, Ont.
1909	Lailey, Walter Whitney, Edmonton, Alberta.
1911	Laing, Allan Victor, Dundas, Ont.
1910	Lake, Walter Edward, Ridgetown, Ont.
1915	Lamont, George A., 22 Liverpool St., Guelph, Ont.
1910	Lane, Richard D. Kinlough, Ont.
1911	Lane, Robert Tarzwell, Sault Ste. Marie, Ont.
1910	Lang, Oscar Kenneth, Granton, Ont.
1909	Langmaid, Clare A., 291 Spadina Ave., Toronto, Ont.
1908	Lannin, G. E. J., South Mountain.
1910	Lannin, John C. J., South Mountain, Ont.
1909	Large, Oliver Sydney, Poole, Ont.
1915	Larocque, Edmond, Alfred, Ont.
1911	Lawson, Alexander Smirle, 28 College St., Toronto.
1908	Lawson, J. H., Brampton.
1912	Leach, William James, North Gower, Ont.
1915	Leacock, Frederick Levi, Easton's Corners, Ont.
1912	Leary, Edgar John, Cooksville, Ont.
1913	Leckett, Warren Frederick, 24 Stuart St., Kingston, Ont.
1912	Lee, John Gagen, Toronto.
1911	Lees, Harry Dewitt, 108 Morrison St., Niagara Falls, Ont.
1912	Legault, Joseph Horace, 82 Church St., Ottawa, Ont.
1910	Leggett, William G., Allanford, Ont.
1913	Leitch, Douglas Burrows, 48 1st Ave. N., South Edmonton.
1911	LeMesurier, Arthur Baker, 63 Isabella Street, Toronto.
1910	Lennox, Joseph W., 108 Simpson Ave., Toronto.
1914	Leonard, Arthur Vincent, 1470 King St. W., Toronto.
1910	Leslie, Norman Victor, 69 Main St. W., Hamilton.
1914	Lewis, Edmund Percy, General Hospital, Toronto.
1914	Lidstone, Arthur Elgin, 157 Division St., Kingston, Ont.
1910	Lindsay, Harry C. D., Strathroy, Ont.
1911	Linscott, Garretson, Brantford, Ont.
1912	Lipman, Arthur, Kingston, Ont.
1914	Little, William Thomas, 389 14th St., Owen Sound, Ont.
1913	Livingstone, Fred Johnston, 182 Sanford Ave. N., Hamilton, Ont.
1915	Livingstone, George Chesterfield, Tottenham, Ont.
1911	Livingstone, Harry Drummond, Listowel, Ont.
1911	Livingstone, John Milton, Baden, Ont.
1911	Lockwood, Ambrose Lorne, Westport, Ont.
1913	Lougheed, Gladstone Wilfred, 675 Bathurst St., Toronto.

1914 Lowery, Bertrand David, 62 Delaware Ave., Toronto.
1911 Lowrie, Andrew, Tillsonburg, Ont. ·
1915 Luney, Frederick Winnett, Grand Ave., London, Ont.
1910 Luton, William Franklin, Mapleton, Ont.
1908 Lyman, W. S., Ottawa.
1910 Lynn, Robert W., Calgary, Alta.
1911 Mabee, Horace Carlton, Odessa, Ont.
1909 Mabee, Oliver R., 136 Albany Avenue, Toronto.
·1909 Mabee, William, 175 Sherbourne Street, Toronto.
1913 Macaulay, Archibald Francis, 118 Wharncliffe Rd., S. London, Ont.
1911 Macaulay, Basil North, Bothwell, Ont.
1910 Macbeth, William Lewis Colquhoun, 60 Brock Ave., Tor.
1911 MacCallum, A. B., Toronto.
1909 MacDonald, Archie, Frankford, Ont.
1915 Macdonald, Joseph Alexander, 12 Maynard Ave., Toronto.
1910 Macdougall, Graham L., 250 McPherson Ave., Toronto.
1912 McEachern, Malcolm Thomas, Fenelon Falls, Ont.
1908 Macfarlane, P. B., Toronto.
1912 MacHaffie, Lloyd, Phyillyss, Cornwall, Ont.
1914 MacIntosh, Aden Floyd, Iroquois, Ont.
1914 MacIntyre, Horace Roy, Kincardine, Ont.
1909 MacIntyre, Reginald Walker, 50 Sussex Avenue, Toronto.
1909 MacKenzie, Charles Roderick, 44 Jackson St., St. Thomas.
1908 MacKenzie, D. W., Toronto.
1912 Mackenzie, Ewen Archibald, 122 Jameson Ave., Toronto.
1909 MacKinnon, Allan James, Star, Ont.
1914 Macklin, Charles Clifford, Milliken, Ont.
1913 MacKnight, Thomas William Fingland, Ingle, Ont.
1908 MacLachlan, J., Toronto.
1911 Maclean, Kenneth Thomas, 534 Princess Ave., London, Ont.
1908 MacLeod, J. A., Priceville.
1908 MacMillan, A. D., Finch.
1909 Macpherson, Fuller S., 72 Elmwood Avenue, London.
1908 Macpherson, G. A., St. Thomas.
1909 Macpherson, William Alexander, Tonawanda, N.Y.
1910 Macy, William J. M., Valens P.O., Ont.
1913 Mahoney, James Leo, Stamford, Ont.
1913 Malloch, Thomas Archibald, 22 Duke St., Hamilton, Ont.
1911 Mann, John Burritt, Bridgenorth, Ont.
1913 Manning, Herbert Kent, 29 Alum Ave., Toronto, Ont.
1915 Marlow, Frederick Charles, Blackstock, Ont.
1911 Marshall, William A., 844 Colborne St., London, Ont.
1912 Martin, Alfred Charles, 173 N. West Ave., Hamilton, Ont.
1914 Martin, Harold Sanderson, 136 Hatten Ave., Hamilton, Ont.
1912 Mathieson, Lily Falardeau Boyington, Port Rowan, Ont.
1914 Matthews, Reginald Allen, 269 Sherbourne St., Toronto.
1912 Mavety, Albert Franklin, Toronto.

1912   Mavety, John LeRoy, Ottawa, Ont.
1914   Maynard, John Cotton, 176 Elizabeth St., Stratford, Ont.
1910   Menzies, Percival K., 25 Charles St. W., Toronto.
1913   Middleton, John Joseph, 102 Gray St., Schenectady, N.Y.
1909   Millar, Adam Hume, Castleton, Ont.
1908   Miller, F. R., Toronto.
1913   Miller, George Robert, 781 10th St. W., Owen Sound, Ont.
1910   Mills, Stanley Gordon, 89 Glen Road, Toronto.
1910   Millyard, Wiley S., Goderich, Ont.
1908   Milne, J. D., Delaware.
1908   Minns, F. S., Weston.
1909   Minthorn, Herbert L., Queenston, Ont.
1912   Mitchell, Elmer Walker, Sandhill, Ont.
1915   Moffat, Ambrose Bell, 68 South Drive, Toronto.
1911   Moffat, Herbert Bayne, 51 Park Ave., Ottawa, Ont.
1915   Monfette, George, 162 Notre Dame de Grace Ave., Montreal.
1911   Montgomery, John Edward, Barrie, Ont.
1911   Montgomery, R. Russell, Wroxeter, Ont.
1909   Moore, Herman Henry, Stouffville, Ont.
1913   Morand, Raymond, 97 Tuscarora St., Windsor, Ont.
1908   Morgan, A. H. E., Moorefield.
1914   Morgan, Charles Richard Llewellyn, 172 King St. W.,
            Hamilton, Ont.
1910   Morgan, Edward A. W., Oakville, Ont.
1915   Morgan, Walter Corneil, London, Ont.
1914   Morrison, Duncan Arnold, Maxville, Ont.
1911   Morrison, Neil Alexander, Elmvale, Ont.
1911   Morrison, Robert Lindsay, 14 Wilton Cres., Toronto.
1908   Morrison, T., Hamilton.
1908   Morrison, W., Ashgrove.
1913   Mossman, James K.
1910   Moshier, Heber Havelock, 14 Pine Hill Rd., Toronto.
1915   Moyle, Henry B., c/o Rev. J. E. Moyle, R.R. No. 3, Water-
            ford, Ont.
1914   Mulloy, Patrick Gannon, Inkerman, Ont.
1908   Munro, N. A., St. Thomas.
1912   Munro, Robert Walter, Uxbridge, Ont.
1913   Munroe, Finlay, Maxville, Ont.
1909   Murphy, Giles Brown, Brockville.
1910   Murphy, Ormond W., Portland, Ont.
1909   Murray, Allister McDonald, 197 Douglas St., Stratford.
1911   Murray, Henry Herbert, 72 Macdonell Ave., Toronto, Ont.
1914   Muterer, Alexander, Ingersoll, Ont.
1913   McAlpine, Gordon Smith, Petrolia, Ont.
1908   McAlpine, R. D., London.
1911   McAllister, Arthur, Hensall, Ont.
1908   McArthur, A. D., Greenbank.
1910   McBride, Chester J., Egbert, Ont.

1908 McBroom, W. T., London.
1912 McCabe, Charles Joseph, 36 Gore St., Hamilton, Ont.
1909 McCabe, Leo George, Waterdown.
1911 McCalla, Arthur Irvine, 113 Ormond St., St. Catharines.
1912 McCallum, John Sangster, Smith's Falls, Ont.
1911 McCammon, John Gordon, Gananoque, Ont.
1910 McCann, James J. F., Perth, Ont.
1908 McCannell, A. D., North Dakota, U.S.A.
1911 McCarley, Ray Vance, Brockville, Ont.
1913 McCausland, Archibald, 92 Metcalfe St., St. Thomas, Ont.
1909 McClelland, William A., Grand Valley.
1913 McClenahan, Claude Andrew, Milton, Ont.
1912 McClenahan, Robert Roy, Waterdown, Ont.
1909 McCormack, Albert M., 39 Patterson Avenue, Ottawa.
1910 McCormack, Victor, Vivian, Ont.
1909 McCormack, W. Gordon M., Vivian, Ont.
1912 McCracken, John Fleming, Brussels, Ont.
1911 McCracken, William Alexander, Cornwall, Ont.
1913 McCulloch, Albert Ernest, Greenbank, Ont.
1913 McCulloch, Charles Douglas, 328 Westmoreland Ave., Tor.
1909 McCulloch, William George, Enfield, Ont.
1912 McCullough, James Stuart, Walter's Falls, Ont.
1911 McCullough, William, 312 Van Norman St., Port Arthur.
1912 McDermott, James Phipps, Eganville, Ont.
1911 McDermott, John Joseph, 266 Johnston St., Kingston, Ont.
1908 McDonald, A., Scotch Line.
1912 McDonald, Ernest Augustus, 608 27th St., Milwaukee, Wis.
1912 McDonald, Marshall, Cowley, Alberta.
1914 McDonough, Vincent Arthur, Nashville, Ont.
1910 McEwen, John A., Hensall, Ont.
1910 McEwen, Robert J., Moffat, Ont.
1908 McFadden, H. M., Millbank.
1911 McFarlane, William Henry, 23 Edward St., London, Ont.
1915 McGanity, Arthur James, 270 Sanford Avenue North, Hamilton, Ont.
1912 McGavin, Edwin Henry, Seaforth, Ont.
1909 McGibbon, James Archibald, Forest.
1908 McGillicuddy, J. E., Watford.
1912 McGilvery, Frank E. Beacham, Simcoe, Ont.
1911 McGlennon, Archibald Campbell, Colborne, Ont.
1913 McIlwraith, Wyatt Lorne, Woodstock, Ont.
1909 McIlmoyle, William D., Bracebridge, Ont.
1910 McIntosh, Frank B., Williamsburg, Ont.
1910 McIntosh, John Hampden, Dominionville, Ont.
1914 McIntosh, William Verne, Box 222, Windsor, Ont.
1911 McIntyre, Edward Lorne, Forest, Ont.
1915 McIntyre, George Crerar, Paisley, Ont.
1910 McInnis, John Archibald, Manilla, Ont.

1911 McKay, Charles Reginald, Port Colborne, Ont.
1912 McKay, Donald George Sinclair, Bradford, Ont.
1914 McKay, Hugh Alexander, 43 Murray St., Toronto.
1911 McKay, Robert Alexander, Ingersoll, Ont.
1910 McKee, James F., 192 Euclid Ave., Toronto.
1909 McKelvey, Alexander Dunbar, Brussels.
1915 McKendry, John Judson, South Mountain, Ont.
1914 McKenzie, Kenneth' George, Monkton, Ont.
1914 McKenzie, Walter Wake, 66 Melbourne Ave., Toronto.
1914 McKibbin, Alan Ernest, Chelsea, Que.
1913 McKillip, Thomas Henry, 11 Sussex Court, Toronto.
1910 McKinley, Nathan J., Seely's Bay, Ont.
1914 McKinley, William Ezra, Toronto.
1911 McLaren, Kenneth Arthur, 141 Laurier Ave., Ottawa, Ont.
1912 McLaren, Laura Merriam, Guelph, Ont.
1909 McLaren, Thomas C., Cobalt.
1915 McLaren, William Russell, Corunna.
1915 McLarty, Gordon Archibald, 70 Kendal Ave., Toronto,
1913 McLay, James Franklin, Woodstock, Ont.
1911 McLay, McMurrich, Woodstock, Ont.
1908 McLean, A. A., Duart.
1913 McLean, Charles Ernest, Athens, Ont.
1914 McLean, William John, Belgrave, Ont.
1910 McLean, William T., 330 Major St., Toronto.
1908 McLennan, A. L., Lancaster.
1914 McLeod, Alex., Bayfield, Ont.
1908 McLeod, Neil, Ottawa.
1909 McMillan, Andrew R., Newark, Ont.
1915 McMullen, David, Petrolea, R.R. No. 1.
1912 McMurchy, Archibald Harry, North Bay, Ont.
1908 McNichol, O. A., Toronto.
1911 McPhee, John Duncan, Brechin, Ont.
1912 McPhedran, Frederic Maurice, 151 Bloor St. W., Toronto.
1911 McPherson, Charles James, Metcalf, Ont.
1914 McQuade, Ernest Alexander, 438 Markham St., Toronto.
1915 McQuay, Jonathan Foote, 105 Howard St., Toronto.
1912 McQuibban, George Alexander, Harriston, Ont.
1912 McQuibban, James William, Harriston, Ont.
1908 McRuer, J. McI., Ayr.
1910 McTavish, Robert, La Vallee, Ont.
1911 McVean, Sarah Georgiana, Dresden, Ont.
1908 McVicar, C. S., Ailsa Craig.
1915 McVicker, Edgar Harold, 855 Manning Ave., Toronto.
1911 Nancekivell, Thomas Wesley, Woodstock, Ont.
1911 Naylor, Archibald Enos, Essex, Ont.
1915 Naylor, Robert White, 568 Spadina Ave., Toronto.
1911 Nelson, Samuel Walter Harper, 307 Crawford St., Toronto, Ont.

1909 Neely, Frederick L., Dorchester Station, Ont.
1911 Nettleton, John Morris, Penetanguishene, Ont.
1915 Newell, Charles, Milton, Ont.
1908 Newell, O. J., Aylmer.
1915 Newman, William Robert, 106 Wilton Ave., Toronto.
1913 Nicholson, Harry Manley, 11 Sussex Court, Toronto.
1911 Nicholson, William Freeman, Dundas, Ont.
1908 Nickle, M. A., Madoc.
1908 Nicolle, F. R., Coe Hill.
1911 Niemeier, Otto Wilmot, 94 Annette St., West Toronto, Ont.
1912 Oakley, Geraldine, Craigville, Ont.
1915 O'Connor, Frances De Sales, Harrowsmith, Ont.
1910 O'Connor, Frederick J., Campbellford.
1909 Ogden, W. E., Gravenhurst, Ont.
1915 O'Gorman, Vincent Keating, Cobalt, Ont.
1913 Oldham, Edmund Morell Alexander, Desboro, Ont.
1912 O'Leary, George Arthur, 145 Margueretta St., Toronto.
1912 O'Meara, Leo Harold, Fallowfield, Ont.
1909 Orok, Robert Dick, Le Pas, Man.
1909 Orr, Thomas Stanley, 166 East Main St., Hamilton, Ont.
1913 Otton, Stafford Walker, Leamington, Ont.
1908 Ovens, A. P., London.
1911 Pain, Alfred, 136 Main St. W., Hamilton, Ont. -
1914 Palmer, Laurel Cole, 217 Jameson Ave., Toronto.
1911 Park, Frank Stewart, 637 Euclid Ave., Toronto, Ont.
1915 Parker, Arthur Allan, Hospital for Sick Children, Toronto.
1909 Parker, Charles Bemister, 43 St. James Ave., Toronto.
1912 Parr, Russell Leonard, Toronto.
1914 Paterson, Murray Hulme, 108 Stanley Ave., Chatham.
1909 Paterson, Robert Hopkins, 38 Grant Ave., Hamilton, Ont.
1908 Paterson, R. K., Renfrew.
1911 Paton, James Paterson, Merritton, Ont.
1911 Patterson, Claude Allison, Forest, Ont.
1909 Patterson, Geo. H., Stella, Ont.
1908 Paul, R. D., Chicago, U.S.A.
1914 Pearce, Leslie Gladstone, 211 Wellington St., Brantford.
1914 Pearse, Robin, 58 Avenue Road, Toronto.
1915 Pearson, Gerald Hamilton Jeffery, 132 Central Ave., London, Ont.
1910 Pearson, W. E., Weston.
1910 Peart, Thomas Wellesley, Freeman P. O., Ont.
1914 Peck, John Wilmer, Seaforth, Ont.
1910 Pedlar, William Clare, Bonfield, Ont.
1911 Penney, William George, 704 Gerrard St. East, Toronto.
1910 Pentecost, Reginald S., 407 Huron St., Toronto.
1908 Pepin, W. C., Windsor.
1911 Pettman, Frank Ernest, Southend, Ont.
1911 Phair, John Thomas, 615 Givens St., Toronto, Ont.

1913	Phelps, Roy Cecil, Merritton, Ont.
1915	Phillips, Robert Wesley, 618 Dovercourt Rd., Toronto, Ont.
1910	Philp, George Rowe, 94 Hess St. N., Hamilton, Ont.
1910	Phipps, Thomas R., 269 Grosvenor St., London.
1914	Pickard, Orlando William, Sandwich, Ont.
1911	Pickard, Thomas Reginald, St. Mary's, Ont.
1910	Pirie, Henry Hampton, Dundas.
1913	Plewes, W. F., 25 McMaster Ave., Toronto.
1912	Platt, Garfield Arthur, Kingston, Ont.
1909	Pogue, Osman Amos, 1466 Queen St. W., Toronto.
1911	Poirier, John Leo, 4 Court St., St. Catharines, Ont.
1915	Poisson, Adelard Louis, Belle River, Ont.
1910	Poisson, Paul, Belle River, Ont.
1914	Pollock, John Melanchton, Berwick, Ont.
1911	Pollock, Maurice Aaron, 386 Yonge St., Toronto, Ont.
1912	Polson, Stuart MacDowall, 317 University Ave., Kingston, Ont.
1912	Poole, Albert Gower, Trenton, Ont.
1909	Pratt, Wallace, Cobourg.
1914	Pratten, Frank Harten, 179 Dowling Ave., Toronto.
1908	Prentice, A. J., Drumbo.
1911	Priestman, Gordon, Marshville, Ont.
1911	Pringle, George Wesley, Madoc, Ont.
1908	Publew, C. A., Ithaca, N.Y.
1912	Publow, George Arthur, 181 Clergy St. E., Kingston, Ont.
1914	Quick, Douglas Absalom, Harrow, Ont.
1910	Quinn, Francis P., 352 Nepean St., Ottawa.
1910	Quinn, James S., Tweed.
1908	Racey, G. W., Kirkton.
1909	Rae, Edgar, Burlington.
1911	Ramsay, George Alexander, West London, Ont.
1911	Raphael, Howard Maclaren, Wakefield, P.Q.
1911	Ravary, Joseph Mastai, St. Amour, Ont.
1914	Reeds, William Robert, Reaboro, Ont.
1908	Relyea, E. H., Cornwall.
1911	Reynolds, Byron Clarence, Cornwall, Ont.
1908	Rice, A. G., West Toronto.
1910	Richards, James Nelson, Warkworth, Ont.
1911	Richardson, Elmer Freeman, Aurora, Ont.
1909	Richardson, Robert Samuel, 401 Parliament St., Toronto.
1915	Richardson, Roy Barnet, 400 Brock St., Kingston, Ont.
1913	Richardson, Stanley Alexander, Wallaceburg, Ont.
1914	Richmond, Lee Anderson, 297 Central Ave., London, Ont.
1908	Ricker, A. C., Dunnville.
1915	Riddell, Andrew Rutherford, 86 Spadina Rd., Toronto, Ont.
1915	Rigg, Dearden, 217 Victoria Avenue, Niagara Falls, Ont.
1912	Rigg, James Frederick, Niagara Falls, Ont.
1911	Riley, Charles Frederick, Avonbank, Ont.

1914   Risbon, Ernest Hulton, 102 Avenue Road, Toronto.
1912   Roberts, Isabella Hay, 76 Pembroke St., Toronto.
1912   Robertson, Herv John, Kelvin, Ont.
1909   Robertson, Lawrence B., Evening Telegram, Toronto.
1909   Robertson, William Alexander, Monkton, Ont.
1909   Robertson, Winfred H., 415 Manning Ave., Toronto.
1913   Robinson, Clifford Kenneth, 247 Queen Street, Kingston.
1913   Robinson, Howard Parker, Kleinburg, Ont.
1909   Rogers, George Westlake, Kingsville.
1913   Rogers, Harold Percival, Toronto.
1911   Rogers, Norman W., Barrie, Ont.
1909   Ross, Allan, St. Andrew's Manse, London.
1910   Ross, Chas. F. W., Peterboro.
1912   Roszell, Austin, Smithville, Ont.
1908   Routley, F. W., Toronto.
1915   Routley, Thomas Clarence, 149 Close Avenue, Toronto.
1913   Rowswell, Arthur Charles, 67 Dewson St., Toronto.
1908   Rowland, C. E., Toronto.
1912   Rowntree, Harold Lee, Weston, Ont.
1912   Russell, Charles Scott, 22 Market St., Kingston, Ont.
1908   Russell, W. G. F., London.
1908   Ryckman, Warren C., Hamilton, Ont.
1908   Sargent, F. R., Kingston.
1913   Savage, Thomas MacDonald, 15 Yarmouth St., Guelph, Ont.
1908   Sawdon, J. E., Mount Albert.
1909   Sawers, Charles William, Brucefield.
1908   Scheck, W. S., Hamilton.
1908   Schinbein, A. B., Listowel.
1912   Schram, John Spurgeon, London, Ont.
1915   Schram, Norman Franklin, 40 Forward Ave., London, Ont.
1915   Scobie, Thomas Jones, Hazeldean, Ont.
1914   Scott, Frank Ramsay, 18 Maynard Ave., Toronto.
1911   Scott, George Orville, 169 Somerset St., Ottawa.
1913   Scott, Ronald Russell, Perth, Ont.
1913   Scott, William Albert, Langham, Sask.
1913   Seaton, Wallace Balfour, Fort Erie, Ont.
1912   Sebert, Louis Joseph, Brooklin, Ont.
1911   Selby, Ernest Raymond, Bradford, Ont.
1908   Seldon, G. E., Ingersoll.
1912   Shacknove, Nathan, 118 Ray St. N., Hamilton, Ont.
1911   Sharpe, Noble Cameron, Hagersville, Ont.
1908   Shaw, Geo. F., St. Andrew's, Que.
1911   Sheard, Charles, Jr., 314 Jarvis St., Toronto.
1911   Sheard, Robert Henry, 56 Grosvenor St., Toronto.
1909   Shenstone, Norman S., 40 Walmer Road, Toronto.
1913   Shephard, Harold Middleton, 69 Walmer Road, Toronto.
1911   Shields, Harry James, 352 Palmerston Boul., Toronto.
1914   Shields, James Douglas, Mount Albert, Ont.

1913 Shields, Ross Lester, 352 Palmerston Boul., Toronto.
1910 Shier, Robert V. B., Kirkton.
1914 Shute, Richard James, Holland Centre, Ont.
1915 Siddall, William Glenn, London, Ont., 94 Stanley St.
1914 Simmons, George Alonzo, Simmons P.O., Que.
1910 Simpson, James A., Sarnia.
1910 Simpson, James S., Maynard.
1908 Simpson, L. J., Thornton.
1915 Simpson, Thomas John, Waldemar, Ont.
1912 Sims, Herbert Leo, Ottawa, Ont.
1911 Sinclair, Arthur D., Toronto, Ont.
1912 Sinclair, Charles Wilfred, Aylmer, Ont.
1914 Sinclair, William Ewing, Meaford, Ont.
1911 Singer-Pullan, Bessie Thelma, 433 Palmerston Blvd., To-
    ronto, Ont.
1911 Skeeles, Leslie Ord Campbell, 1168 College St., Toronto.
1914 Slater, Robert Franklin, St. Mary's, Ont.
1910 Slater, William Dean, 29 Bellevue Ave., Toronto.
1910 Smillie, Jennie, Hensall, Ont.
1913 Smith, Earl Allard, 145 Cottingham St., Toronto.
1915 Smith, Emerson Charles, Chesterville, Ont.
1909 Smith, Estella O., 15 Mansfield Ave., Toronto, Ont.
1911 Smith, F. C. D., Oshawa, Ont.
1911 Smith, Harry Gray, Port Dover, Ont.
1909 Smith, John Masson, Cannington.
1914 Smith, Morley Thomas, Greenbush, Ont.
1914 Smith, Roy Stanley, 457 Wilson St., Hamilton, Ont.
1911 Smith, Sydney M., South Milwaukee, Wis.
1912 Smith, Wilfred Davy, Currie's Crossing, Ont.
1914 Smith, William Adams, Kingston, Ont.
1912 Smith, William Wallace, Guelph, Ont.
1913 Snetsinger, Herbert Allan, Colborne, Ont.
1911 Snyder, Thomas, 1712 Main St., Niagara Falls, N.Y.
1909 Solway, Leon Judah, 58 Widmer Street, Toronto.
1908 Spankie, A. T., Wolfe Island.
1908 Speers, J. H., Toronto.
1911 Spencer, Frank Everette, Box 233, Picton, Ont.
1911 Spohn, Philip D., Penetanguishene, Ont.
1912 Sproule, Herman Frederick, 77 St. John's Rd., Toronto.
1915 Sproul, Melville John, Martintown, Ont.
1908 Sproule, P. J., Listowel.
1911 Stalker, Gordon Berkeley, Walkerton, Ont.
1910 Stapleton, James L., London.
1915 Stark, William Berkeley, 11 Oriole Gardens, Toronto.
1909 Stead, John Hartford, Lyn, Ont.
1915 Steinberg, Archibald, 35 Waterloo St., Berlin, Ont.
1912 Stevens, Rubert Stanley, Delta, Ont.
1911 Stevenson, William Oliver, 905 King E., Hamilton, Ont.

1912 Stewart, Elizabeth Lilian, Aurora, Ont.
1915 Stewart, Henry Archibald, Saskatoon, Sask.
1908 Stewart, J. 'A., Renfrew.
1908 Stinson, S., Brighton.
1912 Stirrett, Robert Roy, Petrolea, Ont.
1915 Stock, Valentine Frederick, Tavistock, Ont.
1910 Stone, James Giles R., Sault Ste Marie.
1914 St. Pierre, Damien, Moose Creek, Ont.
1911 Streight, Samuel J., Oxford Mills, Ont.
1912 Struthers, Ernest Black, Galt, Ont.
1912 Struthers, James Douglas, Port Elgin, Ont.
1914 Struthers, Robert Gordon, 84 Wellington St., Galt, Ont.
1908 Sullivan, J. H., Peterboro.
1909 Sutherland, Charles G., Hamilton.
1910 Sutherland, Jas. W., 162 Waverley St., Ottawa.
1910 Sutton, Albert E., St. Thomas.
1914 Sutton, Harold Chester, Cooksville, Ont.
1912 Sweeney, Paul Joseph, Arthur, Ont.
1914 Syer, Edmund Coulter, Pontypool, Ont.
1914 Taugher, William John, Box 399, Prescott, Ont.
1914 Taylor, Addison, Lynedoch, Ont.
1910 Taylor, Alexander H., Goderich.
1911 Taylor, Harry Alexander, Wallaceburg, Ont.
1910 Terwillegar, Norman L., Oshawa.
1910 Thomas, James Taylor, Edgar, Ont.
1910 Thomas, Roy Hindley, Barrie, Ont.
1910 Thomas, William McLean, Watford, Ont.
1911 Thompson, Alfred Alexander, Waterdown, Ont. -
1909 Thompson, Clarence P., Listowel.
1912 Thompson, Frank Leslie, Uxbridge, Ont.
1911 Thompson, Franklin John, Lucknow, Ont.
1912 Thompson, Howard, Elsworth, Whitby, Ont.
1910 Thompson, John J., 335 Western Ave., Toronto.
1911 Thompson, Sidney Eustache, 162 King St., Kingston, Ont.
1909 Thomson, James, Hastings, Ont.
1909 Tindale, William Edward, 517 Dundas Street, Woodstock.
1908 Todd, R. R., Toronto.
1911 Toll, William Clair, Carbon, Alberta.
1909 Totten, Charles R., Springbrook, Ont.
1914 Tovell, Harold Murchison, Dentonia Park, East Toronto.
1908 Towers, Thomas L., Sarnia, Ont.
1908 Truesdale, F. H., Harrington.
1913 Trow, Charles Edward A., Shakespeare, Ont.
1911 Trow, Emerson James, 76 Queen St., Stratford, Ont.
1908 Turnbull, E. G., Branchton.
1914 Turnbull, James Grant, Fourth Line, Sarnia, Ont.
1911 Turofsky, Harry Alfred, 187 Queen E., Toronto.
1912 Tutt, William Robert, Parry Sound, Ont.

1908   Tye, P. L., Goderich.
1912   Tyrer, Edward Roy, Toronto.
1909   Tytler, William H., Guelph.
1913   Urie, George Norman, Deloraine, Man.
1909   Usher, William Claude, Colborne, Ont.
1911   Valiquet, Michael Ulric, 611 Cumberland St., Ottawa, Ont.
1915   Vanderburg, William Andrew, R.R. No. 4, Cayuga, Ont.
1912   Vaughan, Merritt Carlton, Forks Road, Ont.
1912   Veitch, Ambert Hastie, Port Elgin, Ont.
1911   Vernon, Edward Gladstone, St. Mary's, Ont.
1911   Verrall, Walter Sargeson, Chatham, Ont.
1908   Walker, E. L., Glencoe.
1913   Walker, Frank Muir, Stoney Creek, Ont.
1908   Walker, H., Bealton.
1910   Walker, Melvin H. O., Toledo, Ont.
1911   Walker, R. R., Waterdown, Ont.
1915   Walker, Stanley Arthur, 43 Summerhill Gardens, Toronto.
1913   Wallace, Charles Kenneth, Kemptville, Ont.
1909   Wallace, Frederick Western, Sonya, Ont.
1911   Wallace, Guy Halifax, 3 Hoskin Ave., Toronto.
1909   Wallace, William Gordon, Metcalf, Ont.
1908   Walsh, W. C., Millbrook.
1909   Ward, Charles Byron, Amiens, Ont.
1913   Warren, Donald Alexander, 128 Hughson St., Hamilton.
1912   Watson, Benjamin Philp, Toronto.
1913   Watson, George Albert, 167 Avenue Rd., Toronto.
1914   Watson, William Virgil, 10 Euclid Ave., Toronto.
1915   Watt, George McKee, 132 Park Ave., Brantford, Ont.
1910   Watt, James C., Hawthorne Ave., Toronto.
1913   Webb, Fred Earlby, Aurora, Ont.
1911   Weir, Gordon Sutton, 197 Sherwood Ave., London.
1911   Weir, Thomas Moffat, Rayside, Ont.
1913   Wellman, Arnold Lorne, Central Ontario Junction, via
      C.P.R.
1910   Wells, Edwin R., Barrie.
1910   Wesley, Robert W., Newmarket.
1911   Weston, Frederick William, Campbellford, Ont.
1909   Weston, Rene E. A., Tillsonburg, Ont.
1913   White, George Edward, 142 Ouellette Ave., Windsor, Ont.
1912   White, James George, Mount Clemens, Mich.
1913   White, John Hill, Nottawa, Ont.
1908   White, S. T., Toronto.
1909   Whittaker, Carlton Charles, 66 Wharncliffe Road, Lon-
      don, Ont.
1911   Whittemore, William Lawrence, 154 Carlton St., Toronto.
1910   Whyte, Marchant B., Isolation Hospital, Toronto.
1912   Widdis, John Bowers, Hagersville, Ont.
1910   Wightman, Robert, Lancaster.

1909   Wilford, Edward C., Blyth, Ont.
1912   Wilkins, Warren Edward, Verona, Ont.
1912   Wilkinson, William Morley, Morpeth, Ont.
1914   Williams, Charles Frederic, Cardinal, Ont.
1909   Williams, Garnet W., Aurora, Ont.
1908   Williams, J. A., Ingersoll.
1910   Williams, Llewellyn B., 511 Markham St., Toronto.
1913   Williams, Louis Edwin, Talbot St., St. Thomas, Ont.
1911   Williamson, George Leslie, Peterboro, Ont.
1908   Willinsky, A. I., Toronto.
1915   Wilson, Charles Edgar, St. Mary's, Ont.
1908   Wilson, C. E., Napanee.
1912   Wilson, Cleveland Roy, 350 Annette St., Toronto.
1909   Wilson, Francis Douglas, 227 Robert St., Toronto.
1915   Wilson, Ivan Dolway, 260 Queens Ave., London, Ont.
1911   Wilson, John Cameron, 260 Queen's Ave., London, Ont.
1912   Wilson, John Parr, Palgrave, Ont.
1908   Wilson, N. K., Toronto.
1914   Wilson, Thomas Geddes, Wingham, Ont.
1913   Windsor, Arthur, London, Ont.
1915   Winkler, William Nathan, 18 St. Patrick St., Toronto.
1915   Wolverton, Harold Alonzo, Nelson, B.C.
1909   Wood, James Henry, Glencoe, Ont.
1910   Woodhouse, Catherine Frances, 58 Duke St., Toronto.
1911   Woods, Joseph Charles, Aylmer East, Que.
1913   Wookey, Harold William, 118 Collier St., Toronto.
1909   Workman, Harold C., 113 Alfred St., Kingston, Ont.
1910   Worley, Ernest G., Haley's Station.
1911   Wright, Charles Stewart, Campbellcroft, Ont.
1914   Wright, Clarence Francis, 950 Princess Ave., London, Ont.
1914   Wright, Henry Pulteney, Ottawa, Ont.
1914   Wynne, Charles Stuart, 7 Albertus Ave., Toronto.
1913   Yealand, Louis Ralph, 350 Piccadilly St., London, Ont.
1912   Yelland, Herbert Maxwell, 549 Homewood Ave., Peterborough, Ont.
1909   Yellowlees, Norman J. L., 23 Division St., Toronto.
1912   Young, Clarence Randolph, Guelph, Ont.
1908   Young, E. H., Kingston.
1908   Young, F. S., Seeley's Bay.
1911   Young, Roland Wilbur, Waterloo, Ont.
1912   Zumstein, Ernest William, Winslow, Ont.

IN THIS LIST WILL BE FOUND NAMES OF MEMBERS WHO WERE ADMITTED TO THE COLLEGE, OTHERWISE THAN BY EXAMINATION, AND ALSO CERTAIN NAMES OMITTED FROM THE LAST PUBLISHED REGISTER.

DATE OF REGISTRATION.	NAME.		RESIDENCE.	QUALIFICATION.
1890	May 22—Adams, Ezra Herbert....	11	Toronto, Cor. Queen & Bond Sts.	Mem. Col. Phys. and Surg., Ont., 1890; M.D.C.M., Univ. Vic. Col., Cobourg, 1890.
1890	May 22—Agar, John Samuel	1	Dover Centre	Mem. Col. Phys. and Surg., Ont., 1890; M.B., Univ. Toronto, 1890.
1890	May 22—Agar, Mary Louisa......	1	Dover Centre	Mem. Col. Phys. and Surg., Ont., 1890; M.D.C.M., Univ. Trin. Col., Tor., 1890.
1915	June 9—Allan, Robert	8	Welland, Ont.	Mem. Col. Phys. and Surg., Ont., 1915; M.D.C.M., McGill Univ.; Lic. C. P. and S., Man.; L.M.C.C., 1915.
1915	Allison, Gerald	15	Picton, Ont.	Mem. Col. Phys. and Surg., Ont., 1915; M.B., Univ. of Toronto, 1915.
1900	May 29—Amys, C. H.	14	Ashburnham, Peterboro	Mem. Col. Phys. and Surg., Ont., 1900; Phm.B., Univ. Tor., 1895; M.D.C.M., Univ. Queen's Col., King., 1899.
1887	Jan. 5—Armitage, Jos. Hartman.	5	Waterloo	Mem. Col. Phys. and Surg., Ont., 1887; Cert. British Registration, 1866; Lic. Soc. Apoth., London, 1866; M.D.C.M., Univ. McGill Col., Mont., 1886.
1915	Armour, Robert Stanley	14	Campbellford, Ont.	Mem. Col. Phys. and Surg., Ont., 1915; M.B., Univ. Tor., 1915.

Year	Name	No.	Address	Qualifications
1915	Baby, George Raymond	7	Hamilton, Ont., 475 Main St. E....	Mem. Col. Phys. and Surg., Ont., 1915; M.D.C.M., McGill Univ., Mont., Que., 1915.
1915	Ball, Stanley Stafford	6	Hanover, Ont. ...	Mem. Col. Phys. and Surg., Ont., 1915; M.B., Univ. Toronto, 1915.
1914	Nov. 19—Bean, Sam. Jas. Thomas	3	Byron, Ont.	Mem. Col. Phys. and Surg., Ont., 1914; M.D., Western, L.M.C.C., 1914.
1915	Bell, Arthur McKnight	17	Merrickville, Ont.	Mem. Col. Phys. and Surg., Ont., 1915; B.A., Trin. Univ., Toronto, 1903; M.A., Trin. Univ., Toronto, 1904; M.B., Univ. Tor., 1915.
1915	June 2—Bell, Deloss Everett ..	16	Kingston, Ont., 138 Wellington St.	Mem. Col. Phys. and Surg., Ont., 1915; M.D.C.M., Queen's Univ., L.M.C.C., 28th Oct., 1914.
1883	Apr. 26—Belt, Reginald William..	13	Oshawa	Mem. Col. Phys. and Surg., Ont., 1883; M.D.C.M., Univ. Trin. Col., Tor., 1882.
1883	Nov. 19—Belton, Cassius Wilkinson	3	London	Mem. Col. Phys. and Surg., Ont., 1883; Cert. British Registration, 1882; M.B., Univ. Trin. Col., Tor., 1881; L.R.C.P. and S., Edin., 1882; Lic. M.R.C.P. and S., Edin., 1882.
1913	Nov. 10—Bergeron, Joseph Albert.	9	Mattawa, Ont. .	Mem. Col. Phys. and Surg., Ont., 1913; M.D., Laval Univ.; Lic. C. P. & S., Quebec, L.M.C.C., 1913.
1915	Aug. 11—Bice, Ernal .	3	Clandeboye, Ont...	Mem. Col. Phys. and Surg., Ont., 1915; M.D.,Western Univ., London, Ont., L.M.C.C., 1915.

1869	June 5—Bice, M.	4	Dungannon	Mem. Col. Phys. and Surg., Ont., 1869; M.D., Univ. Trin. Col., 1894.
1901	June 28—Birkett, Fred W.	18	Ottawa	Mem. Col. Phys. and Surg., Ont., 1901; M.D.C.M., Univ. Queen's Col., King., 1898; L.R.C.P. and S., Edin., 1899; L.F.P. and S., Glasgow, 1899.
1914	Sept. 1—Bonin, Adrien	9	Bonfield, Ont.	Mem. Col. Phys. and Surg., Ont., 1914; M.D., Laval Univ., Lic. C.P. and S., Quebec, L.M.C.C., 1914.
1915	Mar. 5—Bowman, James Thornley	3	London, Ont., 509 Ontario St.	Mem. Col. Phys. and Surg., Ont., 1915; M.D., Western Univ., London, L.M.C.C., 1914.
1880	May 20—Boyce, Walter William	15	Belleville	Mem. Col. Phys. and Surg., Ont., 1880; M.D., Univ. Trin. Col., Toronto, 1880.
1914	Nov. 16—Brown, Walter Aloysius	16	Douglas, Ont.	Mem. Col. Phys. and Surg., Ont., 1914; M.D.C.M., McGill Univ., Mont., Que., L.M.C.C., 1914.
1894	May 29—Bull, J. H.	6	Holland Centre	Mem. Col. Phys. and Surg., Ont., 1894; M.B., University Toronto, 1894.
1915	Burwell, George Beatty	16	Renfrew, Ont.	Mem. Col. Phys. and Surg., Ont., 1915; B.A., Queen's Univ., King., 1913; M.B., Queen's Univ., 1915.
1891	May 29—Cameron, William A.	16	Arnprior	Mem. Col. Phys. and Surg., Ont., 1891; Lic. Royal Col. Phys. and Surg, Kingston, Ont., 1891.

1899	Dec. 11—Campbell, James B. .	3	London	Mem. Col. Phys. and Surg., Ont., 1899; B.A., West. Univ., London, 1898; M.D., Western Univ., 1898.
1915	Carr, Leeming Anderson .. .	7	Hamilton, Ont., 415 King St. E....	Mem. Col. Phys. and Surg., Ont., 1915; M.B., Univ. of Tor., 1915.
1889	May 22—Carruthers, John .	9	Little Current, Algoma	Mem. Col. Phys. and Surg., Ont., 1889; M.D.C.M., Univ. Vic. Col., Cobourg, 1889.
1915	Cates, Harry Arthur .. .	12	Toronto, Ont., 249 Dovercourt Rd.	Mem. Col. Phys. and Surg, Ont., 1915; M.B., Univ. of Tor., 1915.
1899	Dec. 11—Cawthorpe, Fred. J.	6	Tiverton	Mem. Col. Phys. and Surg., Ont., 1899.
1913	Nov. 20—Chalmers, Alex. Beaton..	8	Grand View House, Black Creek, Ont..	Mem. Col. Phys. and Surg., Ont., 1913; British Registration, Faculty of Phys. and Surgs., Glasgow, July, 1880; Lic. in Midwifery, July, 1880; M.B.C.M., Univ. Glasgow, Aug., 1880; Univ. State of New York, June, 1900.
1913	Aug. 29—Charland, Louis Cyriaque	18	Ottawa, Ont., 1009 Wellington St.	Mem. Col. Phys. and Surg., Ont., 1913; M.D, Laval Univ., Lic., Col. Phys. and Surgs., Quebec, L.M.C.C., 1913.
1915	Chassels, John ...	11	Toronto, Ont., 30 Bloomfield Ave.	Mem. Col. Phys. and Surg., Ont., 1915; M.B., Univ. of Toronto, 1915.
1913	Nov. 22—Clairoux, Joseph Albert..	9	Sudbury, Ont. ..	Mem. Col. Phys. and Surg., Ont., 1913; Lic., Col. Phys. and Surgs., Quebec, L.M.C.C., 1913.

1892	Oct. 29—Clark, David Andrew...	11	Toronto, Ont., 121 Carlton St. ...	Mem. Col. Phys. and Surg., Ont., 1892; M.B., Univ. Tor., 1892.
1900	June 28—Clark, George L.	3	London	Mem. Col. Phys. and Surg., Ont., 1900.
1904	May 20—Clark, Wm. Fred.......	11	East Toronto, Beach Ave.	Mem. Col. Phys. and Surg., Ont., 1904.
1881	Apr. 30—Clarke, John Gardiner..	6	Meaford	Mem. Col. Phys. and Surg., Ont., 1881; M.D.C.M., Univ. Queen's Col., Kingston, 1881.
1915	Clement, Frederick Walter	15	Deseronto, Ont. ..	Mem. Col. Phys. and Surg., Ont., 1915; M.B., Univ. of Toronto, 1915.
1890	Oct. 30—Clendenan, Chas. W. ...	11	North Tonawanda, N.Y.	Mem. Col. Phys. and Surg., Ont., 1890.
1915	Coatsworth, Richard Colter	11	Toronto, Ont., 296 Parliament St.	Mem. Col. Phys. and Surg., Ont., 1915; B.A., Univ. Tor., 1910; M.A., Univ. Tor., 1913; M.B., Univ. Tor., 1915.
1894	May 29—Coleman, Frank ..	7	Hamilton	Mem. Col. Phys. and Surg., Ont., 1894; M.B., Univ. Toronto, 1894.
1914	Feb. 18—Coulter, Lester McDonnell	12	Toronto, Ont., 179 Walmer Rd. ..	Mem. Col. Phys. and Surg., Ont., 1914; M.D.C.M., Univ. of Toronto, 1899; L.R.C.P., & S., Kingston, 1899; Fell., Trin. Medical Col., 1899; Lic., N.S., Med. Board, 1899, L.M.C.C., 1913.
1915	Courtice, John Thomas ..	11	Toronto, Ont., 27 Sandford Ave...	Mem. Col. Phys. and Surg., Ont., 1915; M.D., Univ. of Toronto, 1906.

1886	Apr. 29—Creeggan, John George.	17 Portland	Mem. Col. Phys. and Surg., Ont., 1886; B.A., Univ. Queen's Col., Kingston, 1882; M.D.C.M., Univ. Queen's Col., Kingston, 1886.
1915	Crews, Thomas Harold	2 Woodstock, Ont., 38 Riddell St.	Mem. Col. Phys. and Surg., Ont., 1915; M.B., Univ. of Toronto, 1915.
1915	Crompton, Chas. Rod. Blackburn..	8 Brantford, Ont., 92 Dufferin St.	Mem. Col. Phys. and Surg., Ont., 1915; M.B., Univ. of Toronto, 1915.
1913	Aug. 1—D'Amours, Jos. Edmond.	Papineauville, Que.	Mem. Col. Phys. and Surg., Ont., 1913; M.C., M.C.P. & S., Que., L.M.C.C., 1913.
1894	May 29—Danard, A. L.	18 Rocklyn	Mem. Col. Phys. and Surg., Ont., 1894; M.B.C.M., Univ. Trin. Col., 1904.
1888	Oct. 31—Dawson, F. J.	12 Toronto, Ont., 320 Palmerston B'd	Mem. Col. Phys. and Surg., Ont., 1888.
1915	Deadman, William James	6 Beeton, Ont.	Mem. Col. Phys. and Surg., Ont., 1915; B.A., M.B., Univ. of Tor., 1915.
1869	May 5—Devlin, James Alphonsus	4 Stratford	Mem. Col. Phys. and Surg., Ont., 1869; M.D., Univ. Vic. Col., 1866.
1889	May 22—Dickinson, George Arthur	14 Port Hope	Mem. Col. Phys. and Surg., Ont., 1889; M.D.C.M., Univ. Vic. Col., Cobourg, 1891.
1914	Nov. 6—Dupont, Joseph Georges.	Montreal, Que.	Mem. Col. Phys. and Surg., Ont., 1914; M.D., Laval Univ., Lic., C.P. & S., Que., L.M.C.C., Oct. 29th, 1914.

Year	Date—Name	No.	Address	Qualifications
1866	June 12—Eastwood, William O....	13	Whitby	Mem. Col. Phys. and Surg., Ont., 1866; A.B. 1849, M.D. 1851, Univ. Toronto; Mem. Coun. Col. Phys. and Surg., Ont., 1872-75.
1914	Dec. 19—Elliott, Lee	2	St. Thomas, Ont., 156 Wilson Ave....	Mem. Col. Phys. and Surg., Ont., 1914; M.D., Western Univ., L.M.C.C., 1914.
1914	June 25—Fleming, Robert Howard	11	Toronto, Ont., 132 Gamble Ave...	Mem. Col. Phys. and Surg., Ont., 1914; B.A., Dublin Univ., 1880; M.B., Dublin Univ., 1882; B. Ch., Dublin Univ., 1884; L.M. Rotunda, 1883; Ex-Assistant Master of Rotunda Hospital, 1884-87; Gyn. Royal City of Dublin Hosp., 1904-1911; Univ. Examiner in Midwifery and Gynecology, Trin. Col., Dublin.
1915	Fraser, Donald Thomas	13	York Mills, Ont..	Mem. Col. Phys. and Surg., Ont., 1915; B.A., Univ. Tor., 1912; M.B., Univ. Tor., 1915.
1904	July 2—Frederick, E. V.	14	Peterboro	Mem. Col. Phys. and Surg., Ont., 1904.
1887	May 11—Free, Edward John	14	Campbellford	Mem. Col. Phys. and Surg., Ont., 1887; M.D.C.M., Univ. Vic. Col., Cobourg, 1887:
1914	Aug. 26—Giguere, Jos. Phidine...		Chapeau, Que.	Mem. Col. Phys. and Surg., Ont., 1914; M.D., Vict. L.C.P. & S., Quebec, L.M.C.C.

Year	Date / Name	No.	Address	Qualifications
1913	Nov. 20—Giles, George Michael...	16	Calderwood, Union St., Kingston, Ont.	Mem. Col. Phys. and Surg., Ont., 1913; L.S.A., London, Eng., 1876; M.R.C.S., Eng., 1876; M.B., Univ. London, 1877; F.R.C.S., Eng., 1889; D.P.H., Univ. London, 1880.
1915	Gillrie, Frederick Russell	7	Hamilton, Ont., 255 King St. W...	Mem. Col. Phys. and Surg., Ont., 1915; M.B., Univ. Toronto, 1915.
1915	Gorman, Morley Edward	7	Oakville R.R. No. 1	Mem. Col. Phys. and Surg., Ont., 1915; M.B., Univ. Toronto, 1915.
1874	May 19—Gray, J. A.	14	Peterboro	Mem. Col. Phys. and Surg., Ont., 1874.
1914	Jan. 15—Gray, James		Toronto, Ont.	Mem. Col. Phys. and Surg., Ont., 1914; M.D.C.M., Univ. McGill, 1883; Lic., C.P. & S., Que., L.M.C.C., 1913.
1898	Nov. 9—Gray, Thomas L.	2	St. Thomas	Mem. Col. Phys. and Surg., Ont., 1898; M.D., Western Univ., London, 1897.
1902	June 19—Grimshaw, Wm. Stafford	11	Toronto, Ont., 1255 Queen W.	Mem. Col. Phys. and Surg., Ont., 1902.
1871	Apr. 12—Hamilton, Alexander ...	12	Toronto, Ont., 25 Bellevue Ave...	Mem. Col. Phys. and Surg., Ont., 1871; M.A., Univ. Toronto, 1869; M.B., Univ. Toronto, 1870.
1915	Hamilton, Harold Parrish	13	Uxbridge, Ont.	Mem. Col. Phys. and Surg., Ont., 1915; M.B., Univ. Toronto, 1915.
1895	May 29—Harris, Fred C.		Cando, N.D., U.S.A.	Mem. Col. Phys. and Surg., Ont., 1895; M.D.C.M., Univ. Trin. Col., Toronto, 1895.
1914	Dec. 7—Harrison, H. Marshall...	14	Cobourg, Ont.	Mem. Col. Phys. and Surg., Ont., 1914; M.D.C.M., Queen's Univ., M.C.P. & S., Man., L.M.C.C., 1914.

Year	Name	No.	Address	Qualifications
1885	Apr. 29—Harrison, Wm. Spencer..	12	Toronto, Ont., 32 Borden St. ..	Mem. Col. Phys. and Surg., Ont., 1885; M.D.C.M., Univ. Trin. Col., Toronto, 1885.
1883	Oct. 25—Hawk, Albert ..	5	Galt.. ..	Mem. Col. Phys. and Surg., Ont., 1883; Cert. British Registration, 1883; M.B., Univ. Trin. Col., Toronto, 1883; Fel., Trin. Med. School, Toronto, 1883; Lic. and Lic. Midwife, R.C.P., Edinburgh, 1883.
1886	Apr. 30—Hay, William Wallis	1	Wallaceburg .	Mem. Col. Phys. and Surg., Ont., 1886; M.D.C.M., Univ. Trin. Col., Toronto, 1886.
1915	Helliwell, Maurice Round	11	Toronto, Ont., 525 Confederation Life Bldg.	Mem. Col. Phys. and Surg., Ont., 1915; M.B., Univ. Toronto, 1915.
1912	Mar. 16—Herbert, Paul Zotique ...		455 West 47th St., New York, N.Y....	Mem. Col. Phys. and Surg., Ont., 1912; M.D.C.M., McGill Univ., Montreal, 1872; L.R.C.P., London, Eng., 1879.
1915	July 5—Hill, Hibbert Winslow...	3	London, Ont.	Mem. Col. Phys. and Surg., Ont., 1915; M.D., Toronto, L.M.C.C., 1915.
1915	Hodge, William Roy	3	London, Ont., 304 Wolfe St.	Mem. Col. Phys. and Surg., Ont., 1915; B.A., Univ. Toronto, 1912; M.B., Univ. Toronto, 1915.
1915	Howitt, John Ranson	7	Hamilton, Ont., 104 George St. ...	Mem. Col. Phys. and Surg., Ont., 1915; M.B., Univ. Toronto, 1915.
1915	Hutton, William Lorne	8	Brantford, Ont., 221 Nelson St.	Mem. Col. Phys. and Surg., Ont., 1915; M.B., Univ. Toronto, 1915.

Year	Name	No.	Location	Credentials
1915	Jeffrey, Edward Shapter	11	Toronto, Ont., 107 Carlton St.	Mem. Col. Phys. and Surg., Ont., 1915; M.B., Univ. Toronto, 1914.
1894	Oct. 19—Jory, Joseph M.	8	St. Catharines	Mem. Col. Phys. and Surg., Ont., 1894; M.D.C.M., Univ. Trin. Col., Tor., 1894; Fel. Trin. Med. Col., Toronto, 1894.
1890	May 22—Kaiser, Thomas Erlin	13	Oshawa	Mem. Col. Phys. and Surg., Ont., 1890; M.D.C.M., Univ. Vic. Col., Cobourg, 1890.
1915	Keillor, Clifford M.	2	Wallacetown, Ont.	Mem. Col. Phys. and Surg., Ont., 1915; M.D., Western Univ., London, 1915.
1914	Apr. 8—King, John W. DeCourcy	14	Peterboro, Ont.	Mem. Col. Phys. and Surg., Ont., 1914; M.D., Trin. Med. Col., Lic. N. S. Med. Board, L.M.C.C., 1914.
1897	Oct. 11—Kingsmill, Harry Ardagh	3	London	Mem. Col. Phys. and Surg., Ont., 1897; .M.D., Western Univ., London, 1895.
1915	Kirkham, Frederick Russell	12	Toronto, Ont., 640 Bathurst St.	Mem. Col. Phys. and Surg., Ont., 1915; M.B., Univ. Toronto, 1915.
1915	July 2—Lacasse, Joseph Henri	1	Tecumseh, Ont.	Mem. Col. Phys. and Surg., Ont., 1915; M.D., Laval Univ. L.C.P. & S, Que., L.M.C.C., Oct. 21st, 1913.
1913	Aug. 26—L'Africain, Eugene		Montreal, Que., 2000 St. Dennis St.	Mem. Col. Phys. and Surg., Ont., 1913; M.D., Vict. Col., L.C.P. & S, Quebec, L.M.C.C., 1913.
1876	Feb. 7—Lake, Charles B.	1	Ridgetown	Mem. Col. Phys. and Surg., Ont., 1876; M.D., Univ. Queen's Col., Kingston, 1876.

Year	Date	Name	No.	Place	Qualifications
1913	Dec. 5	Lamy, Joseph Lorenzo	18	Hawkesbury, Ont.	Mem. Col. Phys. and Surg., Ont., 1913; M.D., Laval Univ., L.M.C.C., 1913.
1913	Nov. 20	Langrill, Edward Rolston		Virden, Man.	Mem. Col. Phys. and Surg., Ont., 1913; M.D., Trin. Med. Col., Toronto, 1900; Lic., N.S. Medical Board, 1900; Lic. Manitoba Medical Council, 1904, L.M.C.C., 1913.
1893	Oct. 10	Lapp, Levi	14	Pontypool	Mem. Col. Phys. and Surg., Ont., 1893.
1895	Oct. 24	Laurie, Chas. Norvel	10	Fort William	Mem. Col. Phys. and Surg., Ont., 1895; Fel. Trin. Med. Col., Toronto, 1890; M.D.C.M., Univ. Trin. Col, Toronto, 1891.
1885	Apr. 29	Leitch, Henry Dousin	12	Toronto, Ont., 592 Spadina Ave.	Mem. Col. Phys. and Surg., Ont., 1885; M.D.C.M, Univ. Trin. Col., Tor., 1885; Fel. Trin. Med. Col., Toronto, 1885.
1890	May 22	Lockhart, George Douglas	13	King	Mem. Col. Phys. and Surg., Ont., 1890; M.D.C.M., Univ. Queen's Col., King., 1898.
1867	Jan. 1	MacAlpine, Robert Smith	1	Petrolea	Mem. Col. Phys. and Surg., Ont., 1867; Lic. Toronto School Med., 1866.
1895	June 14	Mackay, Alexander	12	Toronto, Ont., 203 Euclid Ave.	Mem. Col. Phys. and Surg., Ont., 1895; M.D.C.M., Univ. Trin. Col., Tor., 1895; Fel. Trin. Med. Col., Toronto, 1895.
1901	June 28	MacLoghlin, Fjorde E.	7	Hamilton	Mem. Col. Phys. and Surg., Ont., 1901.

1887	May 11—MacMahon, James A.	8	St. Catharines	Mem. Col. Phys. and Surg., Ont., 1887; M.B., Univ. Toronto, 1887.
1915	Martin, Herbert Carl	7	Hamilton, Ont., 132 Hughson St. N.	Mem. Col. Phys. and Surg., Ont., 1915; M.B., Univ. Toronto, 1915.
1915	Martin, Robert Beattie	3	London, Ont., 268 Ridout St.	Mem. Col. Phys. and Surg., Ont., 1915; M.D., Western Univ., London, Ont., 1915.
1915	Moon, Athol Alexander	1	Cottam, Ont.	Mem. Col. Phys. and Surg., Ont., 1915; M.B., Univ. Toronto, 1915.
1900	June 4—Moore, James	13	Brooklyn	Mem. Col. Phys. and Surg., Ont., 1900; M.D.C.M., Univ. Trin. Col., Toronto, 1899; Fel. Trin. Med. Col., Toronto, 1899.
1913	Sept. 23—Morgan, Vincent Howard		River Beaudette, Que.	Mem. Col. Phys. and Surg., Ont., 1913; M.D.C.M., McGill Univ., Montreal, Que.; Lic. C.P. & S., Quebec, L.M.C.C., 1913.
1915	Apr. 7—Morin, Jos. Hector Gaston	18	Ottawa, Ont., 105 Rideau St.	Mem. Col. Phys. and Surg., Ont., 1915; L.M.C.C., 1914.
1877	May 8—Munro, William Albert	18	Cornwall	Mem. Col. Phys. and Surg., Ont., 1877.
1900	Dec. 11—McCallum, Samuel	6	Thornbury	Mem. Col. Phys. and Surg., Ont., 1900; M.B., Univ. Toronto, 1899.
1915	Feb. 15—McDiarmid, James Stott	2	Ingersoll, Ont.	Mem. Col. Phys. and Surg., Ont., 1915; B.Sc., Arts, McGill Univ.; M.D.C.M., McGill Univ., L.M.C.C., 1914.

1913	July 18—McManus, John Patrick Cantwell	16	Wolfe Island, Ont., Box 109	Mem. Col. Phys. and Surg., Ont., 1913; C.M.M.D., Queen's Univ., 1896; Lic. Med. Council of New Brunswick, 1898; Lic. M.C.C., 1913.
1896	Oct. 13—McMurrich, John B.	12	Toronto, Ont., 80 Keele St.	Mem. Col. Phys. and Surg., Ont., 1896; Fel. Trin. Med. Col., Toronto, 1896; M.D.C.M., Univ. Trin. College, Tor., 1896.
1877	May 8—McNicholl, Eugene	14	Cobourg	Mem. Col. Phys. and Surg., Ont., 1877.
1898	June 30—McNulty, Francis Patrick	14	Peterboro	Mem. Col. Phys. and Surg., Ont., 1898.
1892	Oct. 29—McPherson, Duncan A.	12	Toronto, Ont., 244 Bathurst St.	Mem. Col. Phys. and Surg., Ont., 1892; M.B., Univ. Toronto, 1892; M.D.C.M., Univ. Trin. Col., Toronto, 1892.
1915	McQuay, Robert Whiteman		Foxwarren, Man.	Mem. Col. Phys. and Surg., Ont., 1915; M.B, Queen's Univ., Kingston.
1914	Oct. 30—Norman, James	12	Toronto, Ont., 430 Ossington Ave.	Mem. Col. Phys. and Surg., Ont., 1914; M.D.C.M., Queen's Univ., King., Ont., L.M.C.C., 1914.
1915	O'Connor Francis Xavier	16	Kingston, Ont.	Mem. Col. Phys. and Surg., Ont., 1915; M.B, Queen's Univ., King., Ont., 1914; M.D.C.M., Queen's Univ., King., Ont., 1915.
1915	O'Sullivan, Paul Michael	12	Toronto, Ont., 1155 King St. W.	Mem. Col. Phys. and Surg., Ont., 1915; B.A., Univ. Toronto; M.A., Univ. Toronto, 1913; M.B., Univ. Toronto, 1915.

Year	Name	No.	Location	Credentials
1915	Overend, Samuel Alexander	8	Caledonia, Ont.	Mem. Col. Phys. and Surg., Ont., 1915; M.B., Univ. Toronto, 1906.
1888	May 8—Palling, John Ferguson.	6	Barrie	Mem. Col. Phys. and Surg., Ont., 1888; M.D.C.M., Univ. Trin. Col., Toronto, 1888; Fel. Trin. Med. Col., Toronto, 1888.
1888	May 8—Park, Pryse Campbell	7	Hamilton	Mem. Col. Phys. and Surg., Ont., 1888; M.D.C.M., Univ. McGill Col., Mont., 1888.
1915	Paul, Reginald	4	Sebringville, Ont.	Mem. Col. Phys. and Surg., Ont., 1915; M.B., Univ. Toronto, 1915.
1900	June 4—Peters, J. H.	7	Hamilton	Mem. Col. Phys. and Surg., Ont., 1900; M.B., Univ. Toronto, 1899.
1914	Nov. 6—Phillips, John Gordon	1	Alvinston, Ont.	Mem. Col. Phys. and Surg., Ont., 1914; M.D.C.M., McGill Univ., L.M.C.C., 1913.
1914	May 1—Pickup, William Samuel	10	Fort William, Ont.	Mem. Col. Phys. and Surg., Ont., 1914; M.D., Manitoba, L.M.C.C, 1913.
1876	Apr. 24—Pringle, Albert Robinson.	3	London	Mem. Col. Phys. and Surg., Ont., 1879.
1913	Aug. 5—Quirk, Edward Langton.		Aylmer, Que.	Mem. Col. Phys. and Surg., Ont., 1913; M.D.C.M., McGill Univ.; L.C.P. & S., Que., L.M.C.C, 1913.
1913	Dec. 18—Raymond, Anson Levi	18	Alexandria, Ont.	Mem. Col. Phys. and Surg., Ont., 1913; M.D.C.M., Queen's Univ., L.M.C.C., 1913.
1899	June 19—Roberts, J. X.	12	Toronto, Ont., 63 Bloor W.	Mem. Col. Phys. and Surg., Ont., 1899; M.B, Univ. Toronto, 1898.

Year	Date—Name	Address	No.	Credentials
1892	May 31—Robertson, Peter B.	Newbury	3	Mem. Col. Phys. and Surg., Ont., 1892.
1913	Oct. 21—Rochon, Paul Emile	Clarence Creek, Ont.	18	Mem. Col. Phys. and Surg., Ont., 1913; B.A., M.D., Laval Univ.; Lic. C.P. & S., Que.; L.M.C.C., 1913.
1902	Dec. 18—Rundle, Howard Cecil P.	Brighton	14	Mem. Col. Phys. and Surg., Ont., 1902; Fel. Trin. Med. Col., Toronto, 1901; MD.C.M., Univ. Trin. Col., Toronto, 1901.
1914	Apr. 24—St. Aubin, Jos. Hildedge.	Stony Point, Ont.	1	Mem. Col. Phys. and Surg., Ont., 1914; M.D., Laval Univ.; L.C.P. & S., Que., L.M.C.C., 1914.
1913	Dec. 29—Saunders, Jabez Beer	Brockville, Ont., 65 Pine St.	17	Mem. Col. Phys. and Surg., Ont., 1913; M.D.C.M., Bishop's Col.; M.D., Toki Lic. C.P. & S., Quebec; L.M.C.C., 1913.
1915	Scott, David Emerson	Spry, Ont.	6	Mem. Col. Phys. and Surg., Ont., 1915; M.D., Western Univ., London, 1915.
1914	Jan. 24—Seguin, Jos. Wm. Andrew	Rigaud, Que.		Mem. Col. Phys. and Surg., Ont., 1914; M.D.C.M., McGill Univ.; Lic. C.P. & S., Que., L.M.C.C., 1914.
1903	Dec. 14—Service, Herbert Ezra	Tillsonburg	2	Mem. Col. Phys. and Surg., Ont., 1903; M.D.C.M., Univ. Trin. Col., Toronto, 1902; Fel. Trin. Med. Col., Toronto, 1902; Mem. Col. Phys. and Surg, New York, 1903.
1891	May 29—Shannon, George A.	Sparta	2	Mem. Col. Phys. and Surg., Ont., 1891; M.B., Univ. Toronto, 1891.

Year	Name	No.	Location	Qualifications
1914	Apr. 21—Simon, Keith M. Benoit.	12	Toronto, Ont., 983 Dufferin St.	Mem. Col. Phys. and Surg., Ont., 1914; M.B., Univ. Tor., 1913; L.M.C.C., 1913.
1881	Apr. 30—Simpson, John	13	Lindsay	Mem. Col. Phys. and Surg., Ont., 1881; M.B., Univ. Trin. Col., Toronto, 1881; M.D.C.M., Univ. Vic. Col., Cobourg, 1881; Asst. Physician Asylum for Insane, Kingston.
1914	Oct. 28—Smith, Arthur Lapthorn.	12	Toronto, Ont., 863 College St.	Mem. Col. Phys. and Surg., Ont., 1914; B.A., Univ. Ottawa; M.D., Laval Univ., 1876; L.C.P. & S., Que., 1876; M.R.C.S., Eng., 1878; Mem. Col. Phys. and Surg., Alta., 1913; L.M.C.C., 1913.
1915	Smith, Harry Roy	12	Toronto, Ont., 48 Yorkville Ave.	Mem. Col. Phys. and Surg., Ont., 1915; M.B., Univ. Toronto, 1915.
1914	Nov. 2—Smith, Joseph Neelands.	18	Ottawa, Ont., 15 Cooper St.	Mem. Col. Phys. and Surg., Ont., 1914; M.D., Chicago Col. Med. and Surg.; L.M.C.C., Oct. 28th, 1914.
1877	May 8—Snider, Frederick Samuel	2	Simcoe	Mem. Col. Phys. and Surg., Ont., 1877.
1869	Nov. 24—Stevenson, John A.	15	Trenton	Mem. Col. Phys. and Surg., Ont., 1869; M.D., Univ. Vic. Col., 1869.
1915	Storms, Thomas Harold Douglas.	7	Hamilton, Ont., 53 Bay St. S.	Mem. Col. Phys. and Surg., Ont., 1915; B.A., Univ. Toronto, 1910; M.B., Univ. Toronto, 1915.
1877	May 8—Stuart, William Theoph.	12	Toronto, Ont., 197 Spadina	Mem. Col. Phys. and Surg., Ont., 1877.

Year	Name	No.	Place	Qualifications
1870 Oct.	—Sutton, James ...	3	Clandeboye .	Mem. Col. Phys. and Surg., Ont., 1870; M.D., Univ. Vic. Col., Cobourg, 1860.
1893 May 30	Taylor, Charles John ..	12	Toronto, Ont., 135 Bedford Rd...	Mem. Col. Phys. and Surg., Ont., 1893; M.D.C.M., Univ. Trin. Col., Tor., 1893; M.B., Univ. Tor., 1893; L.R.C.P. and L.M., Edin., 1893.
1886 Aug. 17	Teasdall, Walter John...	3	London .	Mem. Col. Phys. and Surg., Ont., 1886; Cert. British Registration, 1886; M.D. C.M., Univ. Vic. Col., Cobourg, 1885; L. Soc. Apoth., London, 1886.
1882 Nov. 16	Thompson, Sam. George.	11	Toronto, Ont., 239 Jarvis St. ..	Mem. Col. Phys. and Surg., Ont., 1882; Cert. British Registration, 1882; L.R. C.P. and L.R.C.S., Edin., 1882; M.D., Bellevue Med. Col., N.Y., 1880.
1888 May 8	Towle, Robert Elgin ..	13	Pickering	Mem. Col. Phys. and Surg., Ont., 1888; M.D.C.M., Univ. Trin. Col., Toronto, 1888; M.B., Univ. Toronto, 1888.
1871 Mar. 9	Tucker, Milton Mallory.	14	Orono	Mem. Col. Phys. and Surg., Ont., 1870.
1915	Van Wyck, Hermon Brookfield ..	1	Chatham, Ont. .	Mem. Col. Phys. and Surg., Ont., 1915; B.A., Univ. Toronto, 1911; M.B., Univ. Toronto, 1915.
1913 Aug. 11	Verge, Charles	12	Toronto, Ont., 332 Bloor West .	Mem. Col. Phys. and Surg., Ont., 1913; M.D., Laval Univ.; Mem. Col. Phys. and Surg., Quebec; L.M.C.C., 1913.
1915	Walsh, Stanley Young ..	14	Peterboro, Ont., 317 Margaret Ave.	Mem. Col. Phys. and Surg., Ont., 1915; M.B., Univ. Toronto, 1915.

1874	July 18—Watson, John Henry	12	Toronto, Ont., 167 Avenue Rd.	Mem. Col. Phys. and Surg., Ont., 1874; M.D., Univ. Vic. Col., 1879.
1871	June 14—Wells, Samuel Machell	6	Barrie	Mem. Col. Phys. and Surg., Ont., 1871.
1891	May 29—White, Richard H.		New York, 248 E. 34th St.	Mem. Col. Phys. and Surg., Ont., 1892.
1915	Wishart, David Edmund	12	Toronto, Ont., 45 Grosvenor St.	Mem. Col. Phys. and Surg., Ont., 1915; B.A., Univ. Toronto, 1909; M.B., Univ. Toronto, 1915.
1915	Whytock, Harry Wishart	15	Madoc, Ont.	Mem. Col. Phys. and Surg., Ont., 1915; B.A., Queen's Univ., 1913; M.B., Queen's Univ., 1915.
1915	Mar. 3—Wyman, Hiram Beardsley	18	Chute a Blondeau, Ont.	Mem. Col. Phys. and Surg., Ont., 1915; M.D.C.M., McGill Univ.; F.R.C.S., Edin.; Lic. C.P. & S., Que., L.M.C.C., 1915.
1908	July 1—Wyse, G. H.	4	Stratford	Mem. Col. Phys. and Surg., Ont., 1908.

By-Laws of the Medical Council

OF THE

College of Physicians & Surgeons

OF ONTARIO

By-Law No. 1.

Whereas the Council of the College of Physicians and Surgeons of Ontario are empowered under Section 12, Chapter 176, R.S.O. 1897, to pass By-laws and make Rules and Regulations for its government;

Now, therefore, the Council of the College of Physicians and Surgeons of Ontario enacts as follows:

That all existing By-laws of the said Council of the College of Physicians and Surgeons of Ontario be now and are hereby rescinded.

Read first, second and third time.

Adopted July 1st, 1915.

J. Fenton Argue,
Chairman Committee of the Whole.

H. S. Griffin,   H. Wilberforce Aikins,
President.   Registrar.

By-Law No. 2.

Whereas the Council of the College of Physicians and Surgeons of Ontario are empowered, under Section 12, Chapter 176, R.S.O., 1897, to pass By-laws and make Rules and Regulations for its government;

Now, therefore, the Council of the College of Physicians and Surgeons of Ontario enacts as follows:

That all existing By-laws of the said College of Physicians and Surgeons of Ontario be now collected by the Registrar of the said College of Physicians and Surgeons of Ontario and bound in two volumes, which shall be kept in the vault of the said Council of the College of Physicians and Surgeons of Ontario for reference when required.

Read first, second and third time.

Adopted July 1st, 1915.

J. FENTON ARGUE,
Chairman Committee of the Whole.

H. S. GRIFFIN,
President.

H. WILBERFORCE AIKINS,
Registrar.

BY-LAW No. 3.

Rules and Regulations for conducting the proceedings of the Medical Council of the College of Physicians and Surgeons .of Ontario.

Whereas the Council of the College of Physicians and Surgeons of Ontario are empowered, under Section 12, Chap. 176, R.S.O. 1897, to pass By-laws and make Rules and Regulations for its government;

Be it therefore enacted that:

The Council shall hold one session annually in the City of Toronto, commencing on the last Tuesday in June, 1916, hour of two o'clock in the afternoon. The Executive Committee may at any time call a special session, and it shall be the duty of the President to call a special session upon receiving a requisition on that. behalf, signed by not less than one-half of the members of the Council. No business shall be taken up at a special session except that for which the session has been called, and of which each member has been notified.

SECTION 2.—OFFICERS.

1. The Officers of the Council shall be a President, Vice-President, Registrar-Treasurer, Public Prosecutor, Auditor and Solicitor, and such others as the Council may deem necessary.

2. The officers shall be elected after nomination by open vote, the vote being taken on the nominees in the order in which they were nominated. In case of a tie the presiding officer shall give the casting vote, provided that at the first meeting of a new Council the tie for the office of President shall be decided by the member present representing the greatest number of registered practitioners. When only one candidate is nominated it shall be the duty of the presiding officer to declare him duly elected.

Section 3.—Organization.

1. At the first meeting of the new Council the Registrar shall call the Council to order, read over the names of the members, and shall call on the Council to elect a Committee on Credentials, and upon the reception and adoption of the Committee's Report the Registrar shall call upon the Council to elect a President. At all other annual sessions of the Council the President (and in his absence the Vice-President) shall take the chair and preside at the election of officers. In the absence of both these officers the Council shall elect a Chairman.

2. The first business after the organization of the Council and the election of officers shall be the appointment of a Committee to nominate the Standing Committee.

Section 4.—Committees.

1. The Standing Committees shall be the following:
(a) Registration, consisting of five members.
(b) Education, consisting of nine members.
(c) Finance, consisting of five members.
(d) Rules and Regulations, consisting of seven members.
(e) On Complaints, consisting of five members.
(f) On Property and Printing, consisting of five members.
And the following Statutory Committees:
(g) Executive, consisting of three members.
(h) On Discipline, consisting of not less than three members.

2. The President and Vice-President shall be *ex officio* members of all committees of the Council, standing and special, except Committee on Discipline and Executive Committee.

3. A majority of the members of any committee shall constitute a quorum, providing that the said quorum be not less than three members.

Section 5.—Rules of Order.

1. The President shall preside at all meetings (except as otherwise directed in clause 2 of section 2), call the Council to order at the hour appointed, cause the minutes of preceding meeting to be read, confirmed and signed.

2. In the absence of the President, the Vice-President shall discharge the duties of the President, and in the absence of both a Chairman *pro tem* shall be chosen by the Council.

3. The presiding officer shall preserve order and decorum during each session of the Council, and protect the members in the

enjoyment of their rights and privileges. He shall decide all questions of order, giving his reasons for such decision, and citing the rule applicable to the case, subject, however, to an appeal to the Council, and in case of an appeal it shall be put by the presiding officer in the following words: ''Shall the chair be sustained?''

4. All questions of order upon which an appeal has been made from the decision of the presiding officer shall be decided by a direct vote of the Council, without debate.

5. The presiding officer shall declare all votes; but, if any members demand it, such presiding officer, without further debate on the question, shall require the members voting in the affirmative and negative, respectively, to stand until they are counted, and he shall then declare the result. At the request of any two members the yeas and nays shall be taken and recorded.

6. The presiding officer shall not give any other than a casting vote, but he may express his opinion on any subject under debate, and when so doing he shall leave the chair.

7. The presiding officer shall consider a motion to adjourn as always in order; but no second motion to the same effect shall be made until after some intermediate business has been transacted. This motion must be put without debate.

Section 6.—Members Speaking.

1. When any member is about to speak in debate he shall rise in his place and address the presiding officer, confining himself to the question under debate, and avoiding personalities.

2. When two or more members rise at the same time the presiding officer shall name the member who is first to speak.

3. No member, while speaking, shall be interrupted by another, except upon a point of order, or for the purpose of explanation. The member so arising shall confine himself strictly to the point of order, or the explanation.

4. If any member, in speaking or otherwise, transgress the rules, the presiding officer shall, or any member may, call him to order, in which case the member so called shall immediately sit down, unless permitted to explain.

5. No member shall speak more than once upon any motion, except the proposer of the substantive motion, who shall be permitted to reply; nor shall any member speak longer than a quarter of an hour on the same question without the permission of the Council, except in explanation, and he must then not introduce new matter.

6. Any member of the Council may require the question

under discussion to be read at any time of the debate, but not so as to interrupt the speaker.

7. When the matter under consideration contains distinct propositions, under the request of any member, the vote upon each proposition shall be taken separately.

8. No member shall speak to any question after the same has been put by the presiding officer.

9. Notices shall be given of all motions for introducing new matter other than matters of privilege and petitions at a previous meeting to that at which it comes up for discussion, unless dispensed with by a two-thirds vote of the members present. Any matter when once decided by the Council shall not be reintroduced during that session, unless by a two-thirds vote of the Council then present.

10. A motion must be put in writing and seconded before it is stated by the presiding officer, and then shall be disposed of only by a vote of the Council, unless the mover, by permission of the Council, withdraws it. Every member present shall vote unless excused by the Council.

11. At the close of the annual session the minutes of the last meeting shall be read, approved and signed by the presiding officer.

12. In all cases not provided for by these rules, resort shall be had to the procedure of Parliament.

13. The Registrar shall make a list of all motions and reports on the table, in the order in which they were received, which shall be considered the "General Orders of the Day." The order of the same to be as follows:

SECTION 7.—GENERAL ORDERS OF THE DAY.

1. Calling names of members and marking them as present or absent.

2. Reading of the Minutes.

3. Reading of communications, petitions, etc.

4. Reception of reports of Committees.

5. Notices of motion.

6. Motions of which notice has been given at a previous meeting.

7. Inquiries.

8. Consideration of reports.

9. Unfinished business from previous meeting.

10. Miscellaneous business.

All resolutions and reports must be taken up as they appear in the Order of the Day, and no variation of the foregoing order of business shall be permitted, except by consent of the Council.

SECTION 8.—MOTIONS AND QUESTIONS.

1. No motion except to adjourn shall be introduced unless the same be written in ink and contains the names of the mover and seconder.

2. Every motion shall be read by the mover, standing in his place; thereafter it shall be handed to the presiding officer, who shall read and submit it to the Council.

3. When a question is under debate, no other motion shall be entertained except a motion to amend, to commit, to postpone, or to lay on the table, or a motion for the previous question, or for adjournment, which last shall always be in order, except when the Council is in Committee of the Whole.

4. Amendments, whether in Committee or in Council, shall be submitted to the vote before the original motion, in the inverse order in which they are moved.

5. A motion for commitment, until it is decided, shall preclude all amendments to the main question.

6. A motion to postpone shall include a day to be named for the further consideration of the question.

7. A motion to lay on the table shall be taken without debate; when it prevails the subject matter shall not be revived during the session except by a two-thirds vote of the Council.

8. The "previous questions," until it is decided, shall preclude all amendments of the main question, and shall be put, without debate, in the following words: "Shall the main question be now put?" If this motion be resolved in the affirmative, the original question is to be put forthwith, without any amendments or debate.

9. Whenever the presiding officer shall consider that a motion in possession of the Council is contrary to the rules of the Council, or inconsistent with the report or other matter to which it was intended to refer, it shall be his duty to rule it out of order.

SECTION 9.—COMMITTEES.

1. When a committee presents its report it shall be received without motion or debate. On reaching the order of business, "The Consideration of Reports," the reports previously received shall be taken up in order of their reception, and may be acted on

directly by the Council, or referred to the Committee of the Whole.

2. On motion of any member the Council may resolve itself into a Committee of the Whole for the consideration of a by-law, report or other matter, when the presiding officer shall leave the chair, naming a member to act as Chairman of the Committee. As Chairman of the Committee of the Whole he shall have the same authority in Committee as the President in the chair of the Council.

3. When any report of the Committee of the Whole is submitted to the Council, as provided in the preceding rule, it shall be either adopted or rejected, or referred back to committee with instructions to amend or postpone to a time to be fixed for asking the concurrence of the Council.

4. The rules of this Council shall be observed in Committee of the Whole, except the rules respecting the yeas and nays and limiting the number of times of speaking; and the motion for the previous question or for an adjournment can be received; but a member may at any time move that the committee now rise, or that it shall rise and report progress.

5. On motion in committee to rise, or to rise and report progress, the question shall be decided without debate.

6. Committees appointed to report on any subject referred to them by the Council shall report a statement of facts and also their opinion thereon in writing, and it shall be the duty of the Chairman to sign and present the report.

7. All petitions and communications on this subject within the cognizance of the standing committee shall, on presentation, be referred by the presiding officer to the proper committee without any motion; but it shall be competent for the Council by a two-thirds vote, to enter upon the immediate consideration thereof.

8. Every member who shall introduce a petition or motion upon any subject which may be referred to a select committee appointed to consider such motion or petition, shall during the sittings of the Council be one of the committee, without being named by the Council, and shall be the convener of the said committee.

9. Any member of the Council may be placed upon a committee notwithstanding the absence of such member at the time of his being named to such a committee.

Section 10.—Duties of the Committees.

1. *Educational Committee.*—The Educational Committee shall have supervision of the curriculum and all matter pertaining thereto, and to the examination of those who seek for registration.

2. *Financial Committee.*—The Financial Committee shall have the supervision of the fiscal concerns of the Council, and report the condition of the various funds. It shall prepare and report a detailed statement of the estimates required by the Council. It shall consider and report on all matters referred to the committee by the Council.

3. *Registration Committee.*—The Registration Committee shall examine and report upon all applications for registration as matriculates or as practitioners. It shall also examine the registers pertaining to the same, and all matters generally concerning registration.

4. *Complaints Committee.*—The Complaints Committee shall deal with all appeals against the decision of the examiners, and complaints against the Council or its officers.

5. *Property and Printing Committee.*—The Property and Printing Committee shall supervise all matters pertaining to the College Building and its requirements, and shall have supervision over all stenographic work and printing required by the Council.

6. *Rules and Regulations.*—The Rules and Regulations Committee shall consider all matters pertaining to the rules and regulations of the Council.

7. *Discipline Committee.*—The Discipline Committee shall consider all complaints against members of the College of Physicians and Surgeons that may be referred to it by the Council, and shall be governed in its procedure by the Statute in that behalf.

8. *Executive Committee.*—The Executive Committee shall take cognizance of, and action upon, all such matters as may require immediate interference or attention between the adjournment of the Council and the next meeting.

Section 11.—By-Laws.

1. Every Bill shall be introduced, upon motion for leave, specifying the title of the Bill, or, upon motion, to appoint a committee to prepare and bring in a Bill.

2. No Bills shall be introduced either in blank or imperfect shape.

3. Every Bill shall receive three several readings.

4. The question that this Bill is now read a first time shall be decided without amendment or debate, and every Bill, after receiving a second reading, shall be referred to the Committee of the Whole.

5. Each clause, the title and the preamble, shall be considered and passed upon in Committee of the Whole, and the Bill shall be read a third time in Council, signed by the President and the Registrar, and sealed with the corporate seal.

6. The Registrar shall endorse on all bills the dates of the several readings, and be responsible for correctness in case of amendment.

Read first, second and third time.

Adopted, July 1st, 1915.

J. Fenton Argue,
Chairman Committee of the Whole.

H. S. Griffin,   H. Wilberforce Aikins,
President.   Registrar.

By-Law No. 4.

That this By-law shall apply to the payment of members of Council, members of Committees, members of Board of Examiners and Officials.

Whereas, power has been granted to the Medical Council of the College of Physicians and Surgeons of Ontario to fix the amount to be paid to its members and officers under sections 12 and 13 of the Ontario Medical Act, be it therefore enacted, and it is hereby enacted:

1. That the Sessional indemnity for members this Session be $100, together with $10 for every half-day occupied in travelling from their place of residence to the place of meeting, and return, in addition to mileage at the rate of 5 cents a mile to and from the place of residence, the usual deduction at the rate of $10 per half day being made for absence from meeting.

2. That each member of the Discipline Committee shall be paid the same amount per half day and mileage as is paid members of this Council at its meetings.

3. That members of Committees, other than Discipline Committee, when meeting during the recess of the Council, shall be paid a per diem allowance of $15.00 and $7.50 for each half day, and five cents per mile for each mile travelled.

4. That each Examiner shall receive the sum of $20.00, and in addition thereto he shall receive thirty-five cents for each paper he may have to read over the number of fifty at each examination. Each Examiner shall also receive $15.00 per diem for each day's attendance at oral examinations and meetings with the same allowance of five cents per mile for the distance travelled to and from the examinations to place of residence.

5. That the salary of the Registrar-Treasurer be $2,000.00 per annum, to be paid monthly.

6. That the salary of Mr. John Fyfe as Public Prosecutor be $100 per month, to be paid monthly.

7. That the Finance Committee be authorized to elect a Vice-Chairman with power.

8. The salary or fees to be paid to the Auditor by the Council for his services as Auditor be, and are hereby fixed at $75.00.

9. That all By-laws and parts of By-laws inconsistent with the above clause be, and are hereby repealed.

Read first, second and third time.

Adopted July 1st, 1915.

J. FENTON ARGUE,
Chairman Committee of the Whole.

H. S. GRIFFIN,   H. WILBERFORCE AIKINS,
President.   Registrar.

BY-LAW No. 5.

By-law to provide for the election of a territorial member of the Medical Council of the College of Physicians and Surgeons of Ontario, for Division No. 3, to fill the unexpired term of the deceased Dr. James Macarthur.

Whereas, power hath been granted to the Medical Council of the College of Physicians and Surgeons of Ontario to make By-laws to regulate the time and manner of holding the elections under the provisions of the Ontario Medical Act, R.S.O., 1897, C. 176, S. 6, 56 Vic., C. 27, S. 2 (1-2), and amendments thereto, be it therefore enacted as follows:

1. That this By-law shall only apply to the election of territorial representative of the division No. 3, named in schedule "A," and appended to the amended Medical Act of 1893, and for appointing a returning officer for the ensuing election of terri-

torial representative to serve in the Medical Council for the time allotted to him in accordance with amendments of the Ontario Medical Act, as made in 1893, that is to say:

Dr. E. Williams, London.

2. That any member of the College presenting himself for election as the representative of the Medical Council of the College of Physicians and Surgeons of Ontario for a territorial division, must receive a nomination of at least 20 (twenty) registered practitioners resident in such division; and that such nomination paper must be in the hands of the returning officer of the division not later than the hour of 2 o'clock p.m. on the 13th day of September, 1915. In the event of only one candidate receiving such nomination, it shall then be the duty of the returning officer to declare such a candidate duly elected, and to notify the Registrar of the College by sending him such declaration in writing.

3. That the Registrar of the College shall send to every registered member of the College of Physicians and Surgeons of Ontario (excepting only those who are registered as the Homeopathic members thereof), a voting paper (in accordance with the residence given on the Register) in form of Schedule "A" attached to this By-law, and a circular directing the voter to write his or her name as the voter, and his or her place of residence, and the county in which his or her place of residence is situated, and to fill up said voting paper on form of Schedule "A" attached to this By-law, as directed in circular to be enclosed. The Registrar shall, fifty (50) days before the time for receiving nominations for the elections, which time is the 13th day of September, 1915, send a postcard to every registered medical practitioner, excepting the Homeopathic members, in the Province, in accordance with addresses in hands of Registrar, giving the date up to which nomination for representative in the Medical Council of the College of Physicians and Surgeons will be received. The Registrar shall advertise in the Medical journals published in Toronto during August 1915, the fact that an election for the Medical Council is to be held, stating the time that nomination will be received up till, and the time of holding the election. Also a voting paper shall be sent to every registered medical practitioner entitled to receive the same on the third Thursday (16th) of September, 1915, and that every member of the College not having received a voting paper on the 16th September, 1915, when a candidate has been properly nominated for their division, shall send by post to the Registrar his name and address, and the Registrar shall forthwith forward a paper to the member so applying. The voter is to be directed in the circular, which is to accompany the voting paper, to send by post or mail the voting paper, properly filled up, giving the

name and residence of the person for whom he or she votes, enclosed in an envelope, which shall be forwarded along with the circular and voting paper. The envelope in which the voter is to place his or her voting paper shall have the name and address of the returning officer appointed to act in the territorial division in which the voter resides.

4· That the Registrar of the College shall mail the voting paper to the members of the College of Physicians and Surgeons of Ontario, who are legally entitled to vote, according to their address in the possession of the Registrar, on the third Thursday (16th) of September, 1915, the postage, etc., all of which is to be paid by the College, and that the Registrar shall forward to any member making application a voting paper for his division after the 16th of September, 1915, upon application. That the Registrar shall place a stamp upon each of the enclosed envelopes which are to be used by the members of the College in sending their voting paper to the returning officer for the division. That the returning officer shall receive votes sent to him up to the hour of 2 o'clock p.m. on the 1st October, 1915.

5. That the returning officer in each division at the hour of 2 o'clock p.m. on the 1st October, 1915, shall open the envelopes and carefully count and examine the voting papers, and make a record of the entire number of votes cast, together with the declaration of the name of the person and address who has received the greatest number of votes, who shall be declared elected as the representative of the division, and in case two or more candidates receive an equal number of votes the returning officer shall give the casting vote for one of such candidates, which shall decide the election, and then, at the hour of 2 p.m. on the 1st of October, 1915, when the returning officer opens the envelope he has received and counts the votes, all or any of the candidates in the division, or their agents, may be present, if duly appointed and authorized to act in writing on behalf of any candidate and see the envelopes opened and the votes counted, and they shall be permitted to examine all voting papers to satisfy themselves as to the voting papers being properly filled up, and that the persons signing the voting papers were duly registered members of the College of Physicians and Surgeons of Ontario, and entitled to vote at the election of territorial representatives in the Medical Council of the College of Physicians and Surgeons of Ontario.

6. The returning officer in each division shall not open any envelopes he may receive as returning officer until the hour of 2 o'clock p.m., the 1st of October, 1915, and that the returning officers, respectively, shall seal up and return all the voting papers connected with the election to the Registrar of the College within six (6) days from the time appointed for holding the

election, which time is 2 o'clock p.m. on the first day of October, 1915.

That the returning officer shall reject all voting papers that are not properly filled up in accordance with instructions contained in circular which is to be sent with each voting paper.

The returning officer shall return all envelopes received after 2 o'clock p.m. on the 1st of October, 1915, stamped as returning officer of the division, to the Registrar of the College, unopened and marked "too late."

That the Registrar, on receiving declaration from the returning officer, declaring the candidate who has received the largest number of votes in the division, shall forthwith inform the candidate declared elected that he has been chosen to represent said division in the Medical Council of the College of Physicians and Surgeons of Ontario, and the Registrar shall inform the member so elected of the time and place of the first meeting of the Council after the said election shall have taken place.

7. It shall be the duty of the Registrar to attend the said meeting of the Council and to have with him there and then all the papers and documents sent to him by the returning officer in order that they might be submitted to the Council, and the representative so named by the returning officer as duly elected shall form the territorial representative to the Medical Council of the College of Physicians and Surgeons of Ontario for the said Division No. 3.

8. It is hereby enacted that the returning officer of the division is to be named by the Council of the Executive Committee and appointed by the Council, and in case the returning officer appointed either refuses to act or is incapacitated, that the Registrar shall fill such vacancy by appointing some member of the College residing in the territorial division on recommendation of the Executive Committee of the Council.

That the fee for acting as returning officer shall be ten dollars ($10.00).

9. The form of voting paper sent to each member of the College and the form of circular to be used at election of territorial representatives to the Medical Council, is to be the same as that on Schedule "A" and "B" appended to this By-law.

Read first, second and third time.

Adopted in Council July 1st, 1915.

J. FENTON ARGUE,
Chairman Committee of the Whole.

H. S. GRIFFIN,   H. WILBERFORCE AIKINS,
President.   Registrar.

SCHEDULE "A."

College of Physicians and Surgeons of Ontario

VOTING PAPER

Medical Registration Office, University Ave., Toronto.	Election of Territorial Representatives to the Medical Council of Ontario, 1915.
The name of the Candidate for whom your vote is cast . . . . Residence of candidate	I. . . . . residing at. . . . . .in the County of . . . . .do solemnly affirm that I am registered under the Ontario Medical Act; that the signature affixed hereto is my proper hand-writing; That I have signed no other Voting Paper at this election; That I have not voted in any other division at this election; That I am a resident of this division in which I now vote; That this Voting Paper was executed on the day of the date hereof by me. Witness my hand this . . . . day of . . . . .1915. (Signed) . . . .

SCHEDULE "B."

College of Physicians and Surgeons of Ontario.

Election of Territorial Representative to the Medical Council of Ontario, 1915.

The voting paper herewith enclosed is to be filled up carefully, using ink, and put into the enclosed envelope, which is directed to the returning officer, and mailed in time to reach him not later than 2 o'clock p.m., on Tuesday, the 1st day of October, 1915.

Sign your name to voting paper, using ink.

H. WILBERFORCE AIKINS, Registrar,
Toronto, Ont.

BY-LAW No. 6.

To provide for the election of Homoeopathic Members of the Medical Council of the College of Physicians and Surgeons of Ontario.

Whereas power has been given to the College of Physicians and Surgeons of Ontario to regulate the time and manner of holding the election under the provisions of the Ontario Medical Act, R.S.O. 1897, C. 176, S. 6, 56, V. C. 27, S. 2 (1-2), and amended thereto, be it therefore enacted as follows:

1. This Bylaw shall only apply to the election of the Homeopathic members of the Medical Council of Ontario.

2. That the Registrar shall send to every registered Homoeopathic member of the College of Physicians and Surgeons of Ontario, a voting paper and circular, directing each to write his or her name, his or her residence, etc., on the . . . .

3. That on or before a certain time, to be named in the circular sent to each voter, the voter shall send by post or mail to the Registrar of the College, so that the Registrar shall receive the same on or before the . . . . the said voting paper enclosed in an envelope, which is to be sent to the voter, with the voting paper filled up properly with his name and residence, and the person or persons for whom he voted.

4. That the Registrar of the College of Physicians and Surgeons of Ontario, is hereby appointed returning officer for the said homoeopathic elections to take place on the . . . . at the hour of 2 o'clock p.m., and in case a tie occurs, the returning officer is to give the casting .vote, which will decide the election.

5. The said returning officer shall carefully preserve the voting papers sent to him, and shall upon the day appointed, at the hour of 2 o'clock p.m. on the said day, open and examine the said papers sent to him, and carefully count the votes, and make a record thereon of the votes cast, and shall inform by letter the five homoeopathic candidates having the greatest number of votes that they are elected as the homoeopathic representatives in the Medical Council of the College of Physicians and Surgeons of Ontario. And the said returning officer shall, after counting carefully the votes contained in the envelopes, preserve the voting papers and all other documents, envelopes, etc., sent to him connected with the election of homoeopathic members of the College of Physicians and Surgeons of Ontario, and present the same to the Medical Council.

6. The returning officer shall not open any paper or document he may have received as returning officer for the homoeopathetic elections after 2 o'clock on the . . . .

7. The returning officer shall not count any voting paper that is not properly filled out, in accordance with instructions contained in the circular which has accompanied the voting paper when sent to the voter.

8. The returning officer shall permit any candidate, and the agent of any candidate duly appointed and authorized in

writing to act on behalf of any candidate, to be present at the counting of the votes, and who shall be permitted to satisfy himself as to the voting paper being properly filled up, and that the person signing the voting paper was a duly registered member of the College of Physicians and Surgeons of Ontario, and entitled to vote at the election of homoeopathic representatives in the Medical Council of the College of Physicians and Surgeons of Ontario, who may examine any or all of the voting papers.

9. The form of voting paper and circular for the Homoeopathic elections to be the same as that on Schedules ''A'' and ''B'' to this By-law appended.

10. It shall be the duty of the Registrar of the College of Physicians and Surgeons of Ontario to inform the said elected members of the time and place of the first meeting of the Medical Council of the College of Physicians and Surgeons of Ontario.

Read, first, second and third time.

Adopted July 1st, 1915.

J. FENTON ARGUE,
Chairman Committee of the Whole.

H. S. GRIFFIN,
President.

H. WILBERFORCE AIKINS,
Registrar.

SCHEDULE ''A''
Col. Phys. and Surgs., Ont.   Office of Med.
Reg., University Ave., Toronto.

HOMOEOPATHIC ELECTIONS, 19..

The Medical Council of Ontario, 191*

VOTING PAPER

The name of the Candidate or Candidates for whom you cast vote:	Name of Voter .... Residence of Voter...............
1 .... 2 .... 3 .... 4 .... 5 .... Residence	I .... of the ....of............ do solemnly affirm that I am registered under the Ontario Medical Act; That I have not voted before at this election. That the signature to this is my own hand-writing, as witness my hand this............... day of...............1915 (Signed)...............

SCHEDULE "B"

Election for Homoeopathic Representatives to the Medical Council of Ontario.

The voting paper herewith enclosed is to be filled up carefully and put into the enclosed envelope, which is directed to the returning officer, and mailed in time to reach him not later than 2 o'clock p.m. on . . . .

Sign your name to voting paper, using ink.

H. WILBERFORCE AIKINS,
Registrar C. P. & S., Ontario,
Toronto, Ont.

BY-LAW No. 7.

By-law to fix the time, manner and places for holding examinations and appointing examiners.

Whereas, power has been granted to the Medical Council of the College of Physicians and Surgeons of Ontario, under the Ontario Medical Act, to make By-laws, be it therefore enacted, and it is hereby enacted as follows:

That a Spring Examination be conducted in Toronto, and in the City of Kingston and London, beginning on the 3rd Tuesday of May, 1916, and also a Fall Examination to be held in the City of Toronto, beginning on the first Tuesday in November, 1915, in the manner and form prescribed in the Annual Announcement of the College of Physicians and Surgeons of Ontario, and the Examiners for the same be as follows:

Dr. Edwin Seaborn, London, Ont., Surgery.

Dr. Peter Stuart, Guelph, Ont., Surgery.

Dr. W. T. Connell, Kingston, Ont., Medicine.

Dr. J. P. Vrooman, Napanee, Ont., Medicine.

Dr. W. A. Thomson, London, Ont., Midwifery and Diseases of Women.

Dr. F. A. Cleland, Toronto, Ont., Midwifery and Diseases of Women.

Dr. W. A. McFall, Toronto, Ont., Homoeopathic Examiner.

Dr. G. L. Husband, Hamilton, Ont., Homoeopathic Examiner.

Read first, second and third time.

Adopted, July 1st, 1915.

J. FENTON ARGUE,
Chairman Committee of the Whole.

H. S. GRIFFIN,
President.

H. WILBERFORCE AIKINS,
Registrar.

By-Law No. 8.

Whereas the Medical Council, under the authority of Section 6 of Chapter 27, of the Ontario Medical Amendment Act, 1903, adopted Section 27 of the Ontario Medical Act, R. S. O., 1887, Chap. 148 and Section 41a, amending the same, of an Act passed in the 54th year of Her Majesty's reign, Chapter 26, entitled "An Act to Amend the Ontario Medical Act."

And whereas by the said Section 6 of the Ontario Medical Amendment Act, 1893, the Council have power from time to time to make By-laws.

And whereas it is expedient that any member of the College of Physicians and Surgeons of Ontario, who may not practice in any year in the Province, should be relieved of payment of the annual fee for such year.

Now, therefore, the Council of the College of Physicians and Surgeons of Ontario enacts as follows:

The annual fee determined by By-law of the Council, under the authority of Section 27 of the Ontario Medical Act shall not be due and payable by any member of the College who, by reason of absence from the Province, shall in no way practice Medicine, Surgery or Midwifery in the Province of Ontario during the year for which such annual fee may be imposed, but such member of the College shall notify the Registrar that he is leaving the Province, and then notify him on his return, upon doing this, it shall be the duty of the Registrar to exempt him from the fee imposed for that time.

The members so claiming shall prove to the satisfaction of the Registrar that they have not practiced their profession in the Province of Ontario during the year or years for which such fee has been imposed, but shall, if the Registrar requires it, make a statutory declaration to that effect, and furnish such other evidence as may be required.

The decision of the Registrar upon such application as to the liability of the applicant for the fee in question shall be final and conclusive, subject to appeal to next meeting of Council.

Read first, second and third time.

Adopted in Council of the Whole.

J. FENTON ARGUE,
Chairman Committee of the Whole.

H. S. GRIFFIN,
President.

H. WILBERFORCE AIKINS,
Registrar.

By-Law No. 9.

By-law to levy Annual Fee:

Whereas it is necessary and expedient that an annual fee be paid by each member of the College of Physicians and Surgeons of Ontario towards the general expenses of the College, and

Whereas the Council is authorized by Statute to pass By-laws for this purpose,

Now, therefore, the Council of the College of Physicians and Surgeons enacts as follows:

That each member of the College shall pay to the Registrar towards the general expenses of the College for the current year an annual fee of two dollars ($2), pursuant to the provisions of the Ontario Medical Act, Revised Statutes of Ontario, 1897, Chap. 176, Section 43, Sub-sections 1 and 2.

Read first, second and third time.

Adopted in Committee of the Whole.

J. Fenton Argue,
Chairman Committee of the Whole.

H. S. Griffin,
President.

H. Wilberforce Aikins,
Registrar.

By-Law No. 10.

Under and by virtue of the powers and directions given by Sub-section 2 of Section 35 of the Ontario Medical Act, Revised Statutes of Ontario, 1897, Chapter 176, the Council of the College of Physicians and Surgeons of Ontario enacts as follows.

1. The Committee appointed under the provisions and for the purpose of the said sub-section shall consist of not less than three members, three of whom shall form a quorum for the transaction of business.

2. The said Committee shall hold office for one year and until their successors are appointed; provided, that any member of such Committee, appointed in any year, shall continue to be a member of such Committee, notwithstanding anything to the contrary therein, until all business brought before them during the year of office has been reported upon to the Council.

3. The Committee under said Section shall be known as the "Committee on Discipline."

4. Dr. W. E. Crain, Dr. A. T. Emmerson, Dr. Wickens and Dr. S. McCallum are hereby appointed the Committee for the purpose of said sections.

Read the first, second and third time and passed.

1st July, 1915.

J. Fenton Argue,
Chairman Committee of the Whole.

H. S. Griffin,
President.

H. Wilberforce Aikins,
Registrar.

By-Law No. 11.

To appoint an Executive Committee:

Whereas power has been granted to the Medical Council of the College of Physicians and Surgeons of Ontario, by authority of the Revised Statutes of Ontario, 1897, Chapter 176, Clause 15, be it therefore enacted, and it is hereby enacted:

That the Executive Committee for the ensuing year shall consist of Dr. Griffin, Dr. King and Dr. Hardy.

Read first, second and third time.

Adopted July 1st, 1915.

J. Fenton Argue,
Chairman Committee of the Whole.

H. S. Griffin,
President.

H. Wilberforce Aikins,
Registrar.

By-Law No. 12.

Whereas the Council of the College of Physicians and Surgeons of Ontario are empowered under Section 12, Chapter 10, 176, R. S. O., 1897, to pass By-laws and make Rules and Regulations for its government.

Be it therefore enacted that:

Section 1, Clause 1—The Council shall hold the annual session in 1916, in the City of Toronto, commencing on the last Tuesday in June, 1916, at the hour of 2 o'clock in the afternoon.

Read first, second and third time and passed.

Adopted 1st July, 1915.

J. Fenton Argue,
Chairman Committee of the Whole.

H. S. Griffin,
President.

H. Wilberforce Aikins,
Registrar.

By-Law No. 13.

By-law for appointment of Legislative Committee:

Whereas authority is given by the Medical Act to appoint a Legislative Committee, be it hereby enacted that Dr. Ryan, Dr. Addison, Dr. Walters, Dr. Argue, Dr. Routledge, Dr. Cruickshank, Dr. Arthur, Dr. Hamilton, Dr. Jarvis, together with the Executive Committee be appointed, and are hereby appointed for the Legislative Committee for the ensuing year.

Read first, second and third time.

Adopted July 1st, 1915.

J. FENTON ARGUE,
Chairman Committee of the Whole.

H. S. GRIFFIN,   H. WILBERFORCE AIKINS,
   President.   Registrar.

By-Law No. 14.

Whereas the Council of the College of Physicians and Surgeons of Ontario is empowered, under Section 12, Chapter 176, R. S. O., 1897, to pass By-laws and make Rules and Regulations for its government;

Now, therefore, the Council of the College of Physicians and Surgeons of Ontario enacts as follows:

That By-laws Nos. 1 to No. 13, inclusive, shall be standing By-laws and shall not be repeated annually, but shall be modified from year to year by resolution of the Council as to dates and names, and shall retain their original form and number.

Read first, second and third time.

Adopted July 1st, 1915.

J. FENTON ARGUE,
Chairman Committee of the Whole.

H. S. GRIFFIN,   H. WILBERFORCE AIKINS,
   President.   Registrar.

Minutes of Special Meeting

OF THE

MEDICAL COUNCIL OF ONTARIO

DECEMBER, 1914.

FIRST DAY

Toronto, Monday, December 21st, 1914.

The Medical Council of the College of Physicians and Surgeons of Ontario met this day, in special session, at two o'clock p.m., in accordance with the notice calling the same.

The Registrar, Dr. J. L. Bray, called the Council to order.

The Registrar then called the roll and the following gentlemen answered to their names: Drs. Addison, Arthur, Argue, Becker, Brodie, Crain, Cruickshank, Dales, Emmerson, Farncomb, Ferguson, Griffin, Hamilton, Hardy, Jarvis, Johnson, Kellam, King, Macarthur, J. MacCallum, S. McCallum, Routledge, Ryan, Spankie, Stewart, Walters, Wickens, Young.

On motion of Dr. Johnson, seconded by Dr. Kellam, the following were appointed a Committee on Credentials: Drs. Johnson, Kellam, J. MacCallum and King.

The Council then adjourned for a short time to allow the Committee on Credentials to meet and examine the credentials of the members elected to the Council.

Council then resumed.

Dr. Johnson: I have the honor to report, Mr. Registrar and gentlemen that your Committee on Credentials have gone over these papers and found them correct, and I move in accordance therewith, seconded by Dr. King, that the names I now put in be accepted as the names of the members constituting this Council. (Carried).

Homoeopathic Representatives.

Drs. C. E. Jarvis (London), H. Becker (Toronto), G. A. Routledge (Lambeth), E. A. P. Hardy (Toronto), A. E. Wickens (Hamilton).

TERRITORIAL REPRESENTATIVES.

No. 1. Dr. G. R. Cruickshank, Windsor.
No. 2. Dr. G. M. Brodie, Woodstock.
No. 3. Dr. J. Macarthur, London.
No. 4. Dr. A. T. Emmerson, Goderich.
No. 5. Dr. J. J. Walters, Berlin.
No. 6. Dr. S. McCallum, Thornbury.
No. 7. Dr. H. S. Griffin, Hamilton.
No. 8. Dr. E. T. Kellam, Niagara Falls.
No. 9. Dr. R. H. Arthur, Sudbury.
No. 10. Dr. A. D. Stewart, Fort William.
No. 11. Dr. E. E. King, Toronto.
No. 12. Dr. H. J. Hamilton, Toronto.
No. 13. Dr. F. A. Dales, Stouffville.
No. 14. Dr. T. W. H. Young, Peterboro.
No. 15. Dr. T. S. Farncomb, Trenton.
No. 16. Dr. W. Spankie, Wolfe Island.
No. 17. Dr. W. E. Crain, Crysler.
No. 18. Dr. J. F. Argue, Ottawa.

COLLEGIATE REPRESENTATIVES.

Western University—Dr. R. Ferguson, London.
University of Toronto—Dr. J. M. MacCallum, Toronto.
University of Queen's—Dr. E. Ryan, Kingston.
University of Trinity—Dr. A. J. Johnson, Toronto.
Victoria College—Dr. W. L. T. Addison, Toronto.
Ottawa University—Sir James Grant, Ottawa.

ELECTION OF OFFICERS.

The Registrar called upon the Council to elect the President.

On motion of Dr. King, seconded by Dr. Emmerson, Dr. J. Macarthur be elected President until the first regular meeting. (Carried).

The President, Dr. Macarthur, then took the Chair and after having expressed his appreciation of the honor conferred upon him in continuing him in office for another six months said:

Mr. Chairman and Gentlemen: Having been Chairman of your Executive Committee and President of the Council, I consider it my duty to give the reasons for calling this special meeting of the Medical Council. During the last few weeks I have received several communications from members of this Council, and others, have seen editorials in medical journals and newspapers, and a letter from Queen's University drawing our attention to what was supposed to be a handicap to our licentiates who make applications to the British War Office for appointments in the Imperial Army and Navy Service. The Executive also having been called to Toronto re the granting of a charter to establish a school in Hamilton by the Chiropractics, thought well to ask the members of Council resident in Toronto to go to the Government with us, and we took advantage of their presence to consider whether or not it was advisable to call a special meeting of the Council re Reciprocity with Great Britain. Those present were Drs. King, Johnson, Addison and Hart, in addition to those of the Executive, and having obtained all possible available information from our own military surgeons in close touch with these affairs, we felt that not more than perhaps a dozen or so of our men would be affected at present seeking positions in the R.A.M.C. and Naval Service, and we decided that we were not warranted in calling a special meeting. However, from later knowledge we understood other means of action would be taken to bring about reciprocal relations with Britain, so another meeting of the Executive was called, and after considering all the circumstances it was deemed wise to call a special meeting of the Council. The question then arose as to who were members of the Council after December 1st, 1914, and after consulting our Solicitor, Mr. Osler, he gave as his opinion that the members elected on December 1st, 1914, constituted the Medical Council of Ontario. He also informed us that all our officers and committees appointed by the old Council were *ultra vires* after December 1st, 1914, necessitating the reappointment of the officers and committees, and substituting the names of the new Council in place of those not re-elected, or electing new officers entirely, of course these only to hold office until our next annual meeting. Hereafter this difficulty may be overcome by not having our every four year elections until June. So in accordance with all these facts a special meeting is called for to-day for the following purposes, as worded and drafted by our Solicitor:

(1)   To pass upon the credentials of members elected to this Council.

(2)   To elect officers to hold office until the next regular meeting of Council.

(3)   To appoint an Executive Committee, Discipline Committee, Complaints Committee and such other committees of the Council as may seem expedient.

(4)   To consider and act upon the question of registration and admission to practice in Ontario under the provisions of the

Ontario Medical Act of all such persons as are duly registered in the Medical Register of Great Britain or are otherwise authorized to practice medicine, surgery, midwifery in Great Britain upon such terms as the Council may deem expedient.

(5) To consider and authorize such applications to the Legislature of the Province of Ontario as may appear to be necessary or expedient for the purposes above mentioned or in the interests of medical education and practice in Ontario.

On motion of Dr. Stewart, seconded by Dr. Young, Dr. H. S. Griffin, was elected Vice-President of the Council until the first regular meeting.

On motion of Dr. Griffin, seconded by Dr. Hamilton, Dr. J. L. Bray was elected Registrar until the first regular meeting.

On motion of Dr. Ryan, seconded by Dr. Ferguson, Dr. H. Wilberforce Aikins was elected Treasurer until the next regular meeting.

On motion of Dr. Griffin, seconded by Dr. S. McCallum, Mr. H. S. Osler, K.C., was elected Solicitor and Counsel until the next regular meeting.

On motion of Dr. Johnson, seconded by Dr. S. McCallum, Mr. George Angus, C.S.R., was elected official Stenographer until the next regular meeting.

On motion of Dr. Hardy, seconded by Dr. Cruickshank, Mr. John Fyfe was elected Prosecutor until the next regular meeting.

On motion of Dr. Johnson, seconded by Dr. Ferguson, the following were appointed a committee to strike the standing committees: Drs. Hardy, Emmerson, J. M. MacCallum, King, Cruickshank, Stewart, and the mover and seconder.

On motion of Dr. Becker, seconded by Dr. Addison, the Council adjourned for a few minutes to allow the special committee to meet and strike the standing committees.

After resuming, Dr. Johnson presented the report of the special committee to strike standing committees and moved, seconded by Dr. Hamilton, that the report be adopted. (Carried).

The following are the committees:

REGISTRATION COMMITTEE.

Drs. Cruickshank, Spankie, Hamilton, Jarvis, Ferguson.

RULES AND REGULATIONS COMMITTEE.

Drs. Emmerson, Walters, Argue, Crain, Addison, Hardy, Sir James Grant.

FINANCE COMMITTEE.

Drs. J. M. MacCallum, King, Routledge, Kellam, Stewart.

PRINTING COMMITTEE.

Drs. Hamilton, Brodie, Dales, Young, Farncomb.

EDUCATION COMMITTEE.

Drs. Ferguson, Addison, Emmerson, Spankie, Stewart, Ryan, King, J. M. MacCallum, Wickens.

PROPERTY COMMITTEE.

Drs. Johnson, Argue, Routledge, Crain, Walters.

COMPLAINTS COMMITTEE.

Drs. Young, Arthur, S. McCallum, Becker, Johnson.

(The first name on each committee is the name of the person to be the convener thereof).

The Registrar read appeals, as follows:

R. G. Brady, M.B., Toronto; F. W. Brooks, M.B., Toronto; Frank Kelly, Orillia; A. V. Leonard, M.B., Toronto; O. J. S. Little, Toronto; Dr. J. J. McKendry, Brockville; R. W. Phillips, Toronto; T. J. Scobie, Hazeldean; also appeals from William J. Deadman, B.A., M.B., and Dr. Samuel A. Overend, to have their licenses granted; also communications from the Kingston Medical & Surgical Association re reciprocity, all of which are referred to the various committees.

Dr. Ryan then introduced the following motion re reciprocity with Great Britain:

Moved by Dr. Ryan, seconded by Dr. Spankie, that the College of Physicians & Surgeons of the Province of Ontario do hereby affirm the principle of medical reciprocity between Ontario and Great Britain, and that a committee consisting of Drs. J. M. MacCallum, Farncomb, Crain, Kellam, Routledge, Spankie and Ryan be appointed to draft a report giving practical effect to the said principle.

After discussion the portion of the motion referring to the appointment of a committee was withdrawn.

It was moved by Dr. King, seconded by Dr. Stewart that the solicitor, Mr. H. S. Osler, K.C., be asked to state the position of the Council with the Council of Great Britain regarding reciprocity. (Carried).

Mr. Osler then addressed the Council stating the necessary

procedure to bring about reciprocity with Great Britain should the Council express itself in favor of such legislation.

A discussion followed, after which it was moved by **Dr.** Cruickshank that the Council adjourn until to-morrow at 10 o'clock a.m. (Carried).

The Council then adjourned at 5 o'clock p.m.

(Sgd.) J. MACARTHUR,
President.

SECOND DAY

MORNING SESSION.

Tuesday, December 22nd, 1914.

At ten o'clock a.m. the President took the chair and called the Council to order. The Registrar called the Roll and the following members answered to their names: Drs. Addison, Arthur, Argue, Becker, Brodie, Crain, Cruickshank, Dales, Emmerson, Farncomb, Ferguson, Griffin, Hamilton, Hardy, Jarvis, Johnson, Kellam, King, Macarthur, J. M. MacCallum, S. McCallum, Routledge, Ryan, Spankie, Stewart, Walters, Wickens, Young.

NOTICES OF MOTION.

Dr. S. McCallum gave notice that he would move that the report of the committee on prosecutions and infractions of the Medical Act, together with the Prosecutor's Report, be referred to the Executive Committee for investigation, and by them forwarded to the Discipline Committee, if they deem the evidence to warrant an investigation by the Discipline Committee, after the opinion of the Solicitor has been obtained.

Dr. Emmerson gave notice that he would introduce the following by-laws. Nos. 10, 11, 12 and 13.

On motion the rules of order were suspended and the Council resolved itself into Committee of the Whole on the by-laws, with Dr. J. M. MacCallum in the chair.

The by-laws (Nos. 10, 11, 12 and 13) were adopted in Committee of the Whole. The Committee rose and the Chairman reported the adoption of the same to Council.

On motion of Dr. Emmerson, seconded by S. McCallum, the by-laws as passed in Committee of the Whole were adopted by Council and ordered to be signed by the President and sealed with the seal of the College.

The following are the by-laws:

By-law No. 10:

Under and by virtue of the powers and directions given by sub-section 2 of section 35 of the Ontario Medical Act, Revised Statutes of Ontario, 1897, Chap. 176, the Council of the College of Physicians and Surgeons of Ontario enacts as follows:

(1)   The Committee appointed under the provisions and for the purpose of the said sub-section shall consist of not less than three members, three of whom shall form a quorum for the transaction of business.

(2)   The said Committee shall hold office until the next regular meeting and until their successors are appointed; provided that any member of such Committee appointed in any year shall continue to be a member of such Committee, notwithstanding anything to the contrary therein, until all business brought before them during the year of office has been reported upon to the Council.

(3)   The Committee under said section shall be known as the "Committee on Discipline."

(4)   Drs. Young, Emmerson, Crain, and Wickens are hereby appointed a committee for the purpose of said sections.

Read the first, second and third time and passed, December 22nd, 1914.

(Sgd.)   J. M. MacCallum,
Chairman Com. of the Whole.

(Sgd.)   J. Macarthur,   J. L. Bray,
President.   Registrar.

By-law No. 11:

To appoint an Executive Committee.

Whereas power has been granted to the Medical Council of the College of Physicians and Surgeons of Ontario, by authority of the Revised Statutes of Ontario, 1897, Chap. 176, Clause 15, be it therefore enacted, and it is hereby enacted:

That the Executive Committee until the next regular meeting shall consist of Drs. James Macarthur, H. S. Griffin and E. A. P. Hardy.

Adopted December 22nd, 1914.

Read first, second and third time.

(Sgd.) J. M. MacCallum,
Chairman Com. of the Whole.

(Sgd.) J. Macarthur,   J. L. Bray,
President.   Registrar.

By-law No. 12:

Whereas the Council of the College of Physicians and Surgeons of Ontario are empowered under Section 12, Chap. 70, 175, R. S. O., 1897, to pass by-laws and make rules and regulations for its government,

Be it therefore enacted that:

Section 1, clause 1—The Council shall hold the annual session in 1915, in the City of Toronto, commencing on the last Tuesday in June, at the hour of 2 o'clock in the afternoon.

Read first, second and third time, and passed.

Adopted December 22nd, 1914.

(Sgd.) J. M. MacCallum,
Chairman Com. of the Whole.

(Sgd.) J. Macarthur,   J. L. Bray,
President.   Registrar.

By-law No. 13:

By-law for appointment of Legislative Committee.

Whereas authority is given by the Medical Act to appoint a Legislative Committee, be it hereby enacted that Drs. E. E. King, E. Ryan, R. H. Arthur, C. E. Jarvis, G. R. Cruickshank, G. A. Routledge, H. J. Hamilton, J. J. Walters, and the President and Vice-President be and are hereby appointed for the Legislative Committee until the next regular meeting.

Adopted December 22nd, 1914.

Read the first, second and third time.

(Sgd.) J. M. MacCallum,
Chairman Com. of the Whole.

(Sgd.) J. Macarthur,   J. L. Bray,
President.   Registrar.

It was moved by Dr.' Ferguson, seconded by Dr. Addison, that the rules and regulations be suspended during this sitting for the purpose of passing a by-law to fix the time and place for the holding of the next examination. (Carried).

Dr. Ferguson then presented the following report:

To the Members of the Council of the College of Physicians and Surgeons of Ontario:

Your Committee on Education begs to report as follows, re the appointment of Examiners for the ensuing six months.

The Committee recommends the following appointments.

BOARD OF EXAMINERS—January-July, 1915.

Surgery—Dr. Edwin Seaborn, London, Ont.

Surgery—Dr. Peter Stuart, Guelph, Ontario.

Medicine—Dr. W. T. Connell, Kingston, Ont.

Medicine—Dr. A. S. Lockhart, Toronto, Ont.

Midwifery and Diseases of Women—Dr. W. A. Thomson, London, Ont.

Midwifery and Diseases of Women—Dr. B. P. Watson, Toronto, Ont.

Homoeopathic Examiner—Dr. W. A. McFall, Toronto, Ont.

Homoeopathic Examiner—Dr. G. L. Husband, Hamilton, Ont.

All of which is respectfully submitted.

(Sgd.) ROBERT FERGUSON,
Chairman.

On motion of Dr. Ferguson, seconded by Dr. Addison, the report was adopted.

The discussion on the question of reciprocity was again resumed, when it was moved in amendment to the amendment by Dr. Ferguson, seconded by Dr. Hardy, that in the matter of reciprocal registration with Great Britain, this Council shall forthwith proceed to take a plebiscite of the registered practitioners of this Province for or against reciprocity, and in the event of a majority vote in favor of reciprocity the Legislative Committee, under the direction of the Executive, is hereby empowered to obtain from the Ontario Legislature at its ensuing session such legislation as will make reciprocity on equal terms operable between Ontario and Great Britain.

Resolved further that the Executive Committee in conjunction with our Counsel prepare and forward under the seal of this Council a memorial to the proper authorities in Great Britain praying for the removal of disabilities, if any exist, barring our licentiates from the medical department of the Royal Military and Naval Service in Great Britain. (Lost).

It was then moved in amendment by Dr. Emmerson, seconded by Dr. Griffin, that we affirm the principle of reciprocity between Britain and Ontario on the basis of the Medical Register of Ontario and the Medical Register of Great Britain and Ireland.

On motion of Dr. Crain the Council adjourned to meet at 2 o'clock p.m.

(Sgd.) J. MACARTHUR,
President.

AFTERNOON SESSION.

Tuesday, December 22nd, 1914.

The Council met at two o'clock p.m. in accordance with the motion for adjournment.

The President took the chair and called the Council to order. The Registrar called the roll and the following members answered to their names. Drs. Addison, Arthur, Argue, Becker, Brodie, Crain, Cruickshank, Dales, Emmerson, Farncomb, Ferguson, Griffin, Hamilton, Jarvis, Johnson, King, Macarthur, J. M. Mac-Callum, S. McCallum, Routledge, Ryan, Spankie, Stewart, Walters, Wickens, Young.

The Registrar read the minutes of the last session which were confirmed and signed by the President.

READING OF COMMUNICATIONS, PETITIONS, ETC.

The Registrar read communication received from the University of Toronto re reciprocity, which was ordered in the meantime to be filed, and to be referred to a committee, if such be appointed, re the question of reciprocity.

The Registrar read petition from William N. D. Black, Kingston, asking for matriculation, which was referred to Registration Committee.

RECEPTION OF REPORTS OF COMMITTEES.

Dr. James M. MacCallum presented the report of the Finance Committee.

Dr. Cruickshank presented partial report of the Registration Committee.

Motions of which Notice Has Been Given at a Previous Meeting.

It was moved by S. McCallum, seconded by Dr. Walters, that the report of the Committee on Prosecutions and Infractions of the Medical Act, together with the Prosecutor's Report, be referred to the Executive Committee for investigation, and by them forwarded to the Discipline Committee, if they deem the evidence sufficient to warrant an investigation by the Discipline Committee, after the opinion of the solicitor has been obtained. (The President put the motion, which, on a vote having been taken, was declared carried).

On motion of Dr. Ryan, seconded by Dr. Griffin, the matter of Dr. Koljonen was referred to the Executive Committee.

Under the head of unfinished business from previous meeting the question of reciprocity was again considered, when it was moved in amendment to the amendment to Dr. Ryan's motion, by Dr. Cruickshank, and seconded by Dr. Brodie: "That this Council approves of the principle of reciprocity with Great Britain and refers the matter to the Legislative Committee to enquire into and report at our next regular meeting."

The President put the amendment to the amendment which, on a vote having been taken, was declared lost.

Dr. Emmerson's amendment, seconded by Dr. Griffin, was then put to the meeting and carried, as follows: "That we affirm the principle of reciprocity between Britain and Ontario on the basis of the Medical Register of Ontario and the Medical Register of Great Britain and Ireland."

It was moved by Dr. Ferguson, seconded by Dr. Johnson, that the amendment to the motion which was now carried, shall be confirmed as the substantive motion.

The President put the motion, which, on a vote having been taken, was declared carried unanimously.

It was moved by Dr. King, seconded by Dr. Argue, that all preliminary arrangements necessary to bring into force British reciprocity be referred to the Legislative Committee, and that the subject be referred to the solicitor of the College for advice as to the necessity of securing the passage of an enabling clause, and to enter into negotiations with the Council of Great Britain as to terms to enable reciprocity to become effective and report to the next regular meeting of the Council.

The President put the motion, which, on a vote having been taken, was declared carried.

It was moved by Dr. Griffin, seconded by Dr. Emmerson, that all matters pertaining to medical education and practice in

Ontario referred by the last Council to the Legislative Committee be again referred to the same committee with power to take the necessary action thereon.

The President put the motion, which, on a vote having been taken, was declared carried.

Dr. James M. MacCallum read the report of the Finance Committee and moved, seconded by Dr. King, that the report be adopted.

Dr. Emmerson moved in amendment, duly seconded, that the sessional indemnity be ten dollars per half day.

The President put the amendment, which, on a vote having been taken, was declared lost.

The President then put the motion to adopt the report of the Finance Committee, which, on a vote having been taken, was declared carried and the report adopted as follows:

REPORT OF FINANCE COMMITTEE.

To the Members of the College of Physicians and Surgeons:
Your Committee recommend that the sessional indemnity for this session be fifty dollars, along with $20 a day for every day necessarily absent from home in travelling, and five cents a mile.
All of which is respectfully submitted.

(Sgd.) JAMES M. MACCALLUM,
Chairman.

On motion of Dr. Ryan the Council adjourned for one-half hour to allow Committees to complete their work.

The Council resumed at 4.30 p.m.; when it was moved by Dr. Farncomb, seconded by Dr. Arthur, that the property committee take what measures they deem proper in reference to building and equipping a vault.

The President put the motion, which, on a vote having been taken, was declared carried.

Dr. Cruickshank then presented and read the report of the Registration Committee and moved, seconded by Dr. S. McCallum that the report be adopted.

The President put the motion, which, on a vote having been taken, was declared carried and the report adopted as follows:

REGISTRATION COMMITTEE.

December 21st, 1914.

After adjournment of Council the committee met. Members present: Drs. Cruickshank, Ferguson, Jarvis, Hamilton, Spankie and Griffin.

Dr. Cruickshank elected to the chair, Dr. Hamilton acting secretary.

Application of Samuel Overend for registration was heard. No action was taken, committee having no power to register.

Dr. Stewart appeared before Committee in reference to Dr. Koljonen, who is practising in his territorial district without a license. Referred to Prosecutor.

Application of W. J. Deadman for registration was heard. No action taken for the present.

In reference to application of Samuel Overend and W. J. Deadman, Dr. Spankie referred to the fact that the General Medical Council of Great Britain had determined to ask that all making applications for registration because of the war should pass the necessary examinations. As the two cases referred to are similar in character it was thought advisable not to act.

The application of William N. D. Black for matriculation was allowed on his passing his examination in Latin.

There being no other business the meeting adjourned.

(Sgd.) G. L. CRUICKSHANK, H. J. HAMILTON,
          Chairman.   Secretary.

Dr. Young presented and read the report of the Committee on Complaints and moved, seconded by Dr. Johnson, that the report be adopted.

The President put the motion, which, on a vote having been taken was declared carried and the report adopted as follows:

The Committee on Complaints beg to report as follows:

That the appeals of the following are not granted: R. J. W. Brook, F. Kelly, E. F. Brady, O. J. S. Little, J. J. McKendry, R. W. Phillips and T. J. Scobie.

That the appeal of R. V. Leonard was granted and he was given his pass.

(Sgd.) DR. YOUNG,
                    Chairman.

On motion of Dr. Johnson, seconded by Dr. Dales, the minutes of the present session were taken as read, and confirmed and signed by the President.

On motion of Dr. Ferguson, seconded by Dr. Crain, the Council adjourned until the 29th day of June, 1915.

(Sgd.) J. MACARTHUR,
President.

Minutes of the Meeting

OF THE ·

MEDICAL COUNCIL OF ONTARIO

JUNE AND JULY, 1915

FIFTIETH ANNUAL SESSION

FIRST DAY

Toronto, Tuesday, June 29th, 1915.

The Council of the College of Physicians and Surgeons of Ontario met this day at two o'clock p.m., in accordance with the by-laws of the Council.

The Vice-President, Dr. Griffin, took the chair and called the Council to order.

Mr. Angus called the Roll and the following members answered to their names. Drs. Addison, Arthur, Argue, Becker, Brodie, Crain, Cruickshank, Dales, Emmerson, Farncomb, Ferguson, Sir James Grant, Drs. Griffin, Hamilton, Hardy, Jarvis, Johnson, Kellam, King, J. M. MacCallum, S. McCallum, Routledge, Ryan, Spankie, Stewart, Walters, Wickens.

Owing to the illness of the Registrar, Dr. Bray, Dr. Stewart was appointed Acting Secretary on the following motion:

Moved by Dr. Ryan, seconded by Dr. King, that Dr. Stewart act as Registrar for the meeting. (Carried).

ELECTION OF OFFICERS.

It was moved by Dr. Ryan, seconded by Dr. Spankie, that Dr. Griffin be President for the ensuing year.

There being no further nominations, the Secretary put the motion, which, on a vote having been taken, was declared carried and Dr. H. S. Griffin declared elected President for the ensuing term.

The newly elected President then thanked the members of the Council for the honor which had been conferred upon him.

The President then called for nominations for the office of Vice-President, when it was moved by Dr. Arthur, seconded by Dr. Argue, that Dr. Edmund E. King be elected to the office of Vice-President.

There being no further nominations, the President put the motion, which, on a vote having been taken, was carried, and Dr. E. E. King, of Toronto, declared elected to the office of Vice-President for the ensuing year.

The President then stated that the next office to be filled was that of Registrar, and that, on account of continued ill health, the present Registrar, Dr. Bray, had forwarded to him his resignation.

It was then moved by Dr. Hardy, seconded by Dr. Johnson, that the following be a committee to report on the appointment of a Registrar for the College: Drs. James MacCallum, Ryan, Ferguson, Addison, Spankie, King, Cruickshank and the mover and seconder; and that Dr. Bray's letter to the President be referred to this Committee.

The President put the motion, which, on a vote having been taken, was declared carried.

The President then called for nominations for the office of solicitor, when it was moved by Dr. Johnson, seconded by Dr. Jarvis, that Mr. H. S. Osler, K.C., be solicitor to the College of Physicians and Surgeons of Ontario for 1915-16.

There being no further nominations, the President put the motion, which, on a vote having been taken, was carried, and Mr. H. S. Osler, K.C., declared elected to the office of solicitor for the ensuing year.

The President then called for nominations for the office of Treasurer, when it was moved by Dr. Ryan, seconded by Dr. Hamilton, that Dr. H. Wilberforce Aikins, be elected as Treasurer of this Council for 1915-16.

There being no further nominations, the President put the motion, which, on a vote having been taken, was carried, and Dr. Aikins declared elected to the office of Treasurer for the ensuing year.

The President stated that the next office to be filled was that of Auditor, when it was moved by Dr. James MacCallum, seconded by Dr. Dales, that Mr. J. F. Lawson. Chartered Accountant. be appointed Auditor for the year 1915-16.

taken, was carried, and Mr. J. F. Lawson declared elected Auditor for the ensuing year.

On motion of Dr. King, seconded by Dr. Johnson, Mr. George Angus, C.S.R., was declared elected to the office of Stenographer for the ensuing year.

On motion of Dr. Johnson, seconded by Dr. Addison, Mr. John Fyfe, was appointed to the position of public prosecutor for the year 1915-16.

It was moved by Dr. King, seconded by Dr. Johnson, that the following be a committee to strike the standing committees: Drs. Farncomb, Emmerson, Ryan, Dales, Spankie, Hardy and the mover and seconder.

The President put the motion, which, on a vote having been taken, was declared carried.

It was moved by Dr. Ryan, seconded by Dr. Spankie, that the Council desires to express its profound sorrow on the death of its President, Dr. James Macarthur, who, for many years, gave to this Council and to the educational life of this Province an ability of rare merit and a tried and sincere devotion to the best ideals of his profession.

The President put the motion, which, on a standing vote having been taken, was declared carried, and the Registrar instructed to convey the contents of the above resolution to the deceased President's family.

On motion of Dr. King, the Council adjourned for twenty minutes to allow the special committee to meet and name the standing committees.

The Council resumed, when Dr. E. E. King presented the report of the Special Committee, as follows:

The Committee to strike the Standing Committees reports as follows:

REGISTRATION COMMITTEE.
Drs. Cruickshank, Spankie, Hamilton, Jarvis, Ferguson.

RULES AND REGULATIONS COMMITTEE.
Drs. Emmerson, Walters, Argue, Crain, Addison, Hardy, Sir James Grant.

FINANCE COMMITTEE.
Drs. J. MacCallum, Hamilton, Routledge, Kellam, Stewart.

PRINTING COMMITTEE.
Drs. Johnson, Brodie, Dales, Kellam, Farncomb.

EDUCATION COMMITTEE.

Drs. J. MacCallum, Ferguson, Addison, Emmerson, Spankie, Stewart, Ryan, Arthur, Wickens.

PROPERTY COMMITTEE.

Drs. Johnson, Argue, Routledge, Crain, Walters.

COMPLAINTS COMMITTEE.

Drs. Ryan, Arthur, S. McCallum, Becker, Farncomb.

The member named first on each committee to be the Convener thereof.

EDMUND E. KING,
Chairman.

Dr. King moved, seconded by Dr. Johnson, that the report be adopted.

The President put the motion, which, on a vote having been taken, was declared carried.

COMMUNICATIONS, PETITIONS, ETC.

The Registrar read the following appeals which were referred to the Complaints Committee: From Dr. Howard Black, Dr. R. A. Bond, Dr. C. M. Burroughs, Dr. R. M. Cairns, Dr. H. D. Courtenay, Dr. L. C. Fallis, Dr. E. Gardiner, Dr. S. Gelber, Dr. W. C. Haney, Dr. D. E. Lang, Dr. A. G. Ley, Dr. G. C. Livingstone, Dr. H. C. McCaul, W. M. MacKay, Dr. Herbert W. Martin, W. G. Martin, D. Rigg, Dr. J. A. Stewart, W. L. Tyrer and H. C. Allison.

The Registrar read the following appeals which were referred to the Registration Committee: Drs. Adam Ardill, Sgt. F. R. Bailey, A.M.C.; Correspondence from Dr. J. C. Connell, re William M. McLaren, Dr. G. G. Membery, George F. Seaborn, M.D., Dr. M. G. Thomson, C. V. Williams, Thomas S. Winslow, M.D., W. T. Patrick and Charles T. Fenwick.

The Registrar read the following, which were referred to the Finance Committee: Account of Walter R. Campbell, M.A., M.B.; re refund of fees, Dr. J. Thornley Bowman, re refund of fees, Dr. J. S. McDiarmid, re refund of registration fee of Robert A. Wallace.

The Registrar read the following, which were referred to the Education Committee: Re Pharmacy Act; letter from Lieutenant-Colonel F. W. Marlow (this communication was referred to the Registration Committee); letter from Town Clerk of Cobourg, Ontario, re Dr. A. W. Stinson (referred to Executive Committee).

RECEPTION OF REPORTS OF COMMITTEES.

The President presented and read the report of the Fall examinations of 1914 and the Spring examinations of 1915.

NOTICES OF MOTION.

Sir James Grant gave notice that, seconded by Dr. Edmund E. King, he would move the following resolution:

That we, the members of the Medical Council, owing to the great fatality in infant life in this province, are of opinion more care and watchfulness should be exercised in the infant stage of childhood by a special class of trained nurses, and particularly at a time when a large exit of our young generation from Canada is in progress to the seat of war.

CONSIDERATION OF REPORTS.

It was moved by Dr. Ferguson, seconded by Dr. Crain, that the report of the President re Fall examinations of 1914 and the Spring examinations of 1915 be adopted.

The President put the motion, which, on a vote having been taken, was carried, and the report adopted as follows.

Toronto, June 29th, 1915.

To the Members of the Council of the College of Physicians and Surgeons of Ontario:

Gentlemen:—I beg to report on the Fall Examinations of 1914 and the Spring Examinations of 1915:

FALL EXAMINATION OF 1914.

Tried.	Passed.	Failed.
48	22	26

7 Failed on the Whole Examination.
1 Failed on Medicine.
8 Failed on Surgery.
6 Failed on Midwifery and Diseases of Women.
1 Failed on Medicine and Surgery.
1 Failed on Surgery and Midwifery and Diseases of Women.
2 Failed on Medicine and Midwifery and Diseases of Women.

SPRING EXAMINATION OF 1915.

Tried.	Passed.	Failed.
141	96	45

7 Failed on the Whole Examination.
6 Failed on Medicine.
7 Failed on Surgery.

9 Failed on Midwifery and Diseases of Women.
6 Failed on Medicine and Surgery.
8 Failed on Midwifery and Surgery.
2 Failed on Medicine and Midwifery and Diseases of Women.
All of which is respectfully submitted.

H. S. Griffin,
Acting President.

On motion of Dr. J. MacCallum, the Council adjourned to Wednesday, June 30th, 1915, at 10 o'clock a.m. (Minutes approved).

H. S. Griffin,
President.

SECOND DAY

MORNING SESSION.

Wednesday, June 30th, 1915.

The Council met this day at ten o'clock a.m., in accordance with the motion for adjournment.

The President took the Chair and called the Council to order.

The Secretary called the Roll and the following members answered to their names: Drs. Addison, Arthur, Argue, Becker, Brodie, Crain, Cruickshank, Dales, Emmerson, Farncomb, Ferguson, Sir James Grant, Drs. Griffin, Hamilton, Hardy, Jarvis, Johnson, Kellam, King, J. MacCallum, S. McCallum, Routledge, Ryan, Spankie, Stewart, Walters, Wickens.

The Secretary read the minutes of the last session which were confirmed and signed by the President.

COMMUNICATIONS, PETITIONS, ETC.

The Secretary read the following appeals, which were referred to the following committees:

For Complaints Committee—Dr. W. L. Yule, Dr. R. B. Richardson.

For Registration Committee—Dr. L. B. Lyon, for registration as a matriculate; Dr. G. W. MacNeil, for registration as a matriculate.

For Finance Committee—appeal of Dr. D. E. Bell.

Dr. King read request from Dr. Sheppard asking for reinstatement. (Referred to Discipline Committee).

The Secretary read communication re Belgian Relief Fund. (Referred to Finance Committee).

RECEPTION OF REPORTS.

Dr. Emmerson presented the reports of the Discipline Committee.

The President presented the report of the Auditor.

NOTICES OF MOTION.

None.

MOTIONS OF WHICH NOTICE HAS BEEN GIVEN AT A PREVIOUS SESSION.

It was moved by Sir James Grant, seconded by Dr. King: That we, the members of the Medical Council of Ontario, owing to the great fatality of infant life in this Province, are of opinion more care and watchfulness should be exercised in the stage of childhood, by a special class of trained nurses, and thus conserve their lives at a time when a large exit is in progress, from Canada, of our young generation, to the present seat of war.

The President put the motion, which, on a vote having been taken, was declared carried.

CONSIDERATION OF REPORTS.

Dr. Emmerson gave details of the reports of the Discipline Committee re William Macdonald Adams, re Harry Alfred Turofsky, and re Walker's Institute.

On motion of Dr. Emmerson, seconded by Dr. Crain, the reports were received.

On motion of Dr. King, seconded by Dr. Ryan, the consideration of the Discipline Committee's reports was referred to Thursday morning's session.

The Auditor's report was referred to the Finance Committee.

On motion of Dr. Ryan the Council adjourned to meet at two o'clock p.m.

Minutes approved.

H. S. GRIFFIN,
President.

AFTERNOON SESSION.

The Council met at two o'clock p.m. in accordance with the motion for adjournment.

The President took the Chair and called the Council to order.

The Secretary called the Roll and the following members answered to their names: Drs. Addison, Arthur, Argue, Becker; Brodie, Crain, Cruickshank, Dales, Emmerson, Farncomb, Ferguson, Sir James Grant, Drs. Griffin, Hamilton, Hardy, Jarvis, Johnson, Kellam, King, J. MacCallum, S. McCallum, Routledge, Ryan, Spankie, Stewart, Walters, Wickens.

The Secretary read the minutes of the last session, which were confirmed and signed by the President.

Communications, Petitions, Etc.

The Secretary read appeal of Dr. O. J. S. Little, which was referred to the Complaints Committee.

Reception of Reports of Committee.

Dr. King presented the report of Legislation Committee on Reciprocity with Great Britain.

Dr. Hardy presented the report of the Executive Committee.

Notices of Motion.

Dr. Brodie gave notice, seconded by Dr. Dales, that he would move the following resolution: That the Legislative Committee secure an amendment to the Public Health Act as follows: "In all cases of death, where the deceased had been attended by an unlicensed practitioner, it shall be the duty of the regular physician, if the death takes place within ten days of said attendance, to report the death to the Coroner for investigation."

Enquiries.

Dr. Dales enquired re unsatisfactory condition of Ontario Medical Register, and as to members in default of fees, and their names still remaining on Register.

Consideration of Reports.

Dr. Hardy read the report of the Executive Committee and moved its adoption, seconded by Dr. King.

The President put the motion, which, on a vote having been taken, was carried and the report declared adopted, as follows:

The Executive Committee of the Council of the College of Physicians and Surgeons of Ontario held two meetings during the year to consider the question of Reciprocity with Great Britain, as concerned in granting licenses to those enlisting for Overseas Service in the Canadian Expeditionary Forces, and who were qualified to take the examination of the Council, and who have otherwise fulfilled all the requirements of the Council.

In consideration of the fact that these students were required to leave the country before the time appointed for the final examination, it was decided to grant them licenses on payment of the required fee, and on presenting certificates from commanding officers that they were bona fide members of the said expeditionary forces.

· Herbert Carl Martin was granted his Matriculation Registration for the same reason.

Re E. Gardiner, it was decided not to grant the license, but he was advised to petition the Council at its next meeting.

Re W. S. Downham's application for license not granted, as he is not properly qualified and has not fulfilled the requirements.

The Registrar was granted a short holiday to enable him to recover from his latest severe illness.

The following are the names of those who were granted licenses:

Allison, Gerald, Picton, Ont.
Armour, Robert Stanley, Campbellford, Ont.
Baby, George Raymond, Hamilton, Ontario.
Ball, Stanley Stafford, Hanover, Ont.
Bell, Arthur McKnight, Merrickville, Ont.
Burwell, George Beatty, Renfrew, Ont.
Carr, Leeming Anderson, Hamilton, Ont., 415 King St. E.
Cates, Harry Arthur, Toronto, Ont., 249 Dovercourt Rd.
Chassels, John, Toronto, Ont., 30 Bloomfield Ave.
Clement, Frederick Walter, Deseronto, Ont.
Coatsworth, Richard Colter, Toronto, Ont., 296 Parliament St.
Courtice, John Thomas, Toronto, Ont., 27 Sandford Ave.
Crews, Thomas Harold, Woodstock, Ont., 38 Riddell St.
Crompton, Charles Roderick Blackburn, Brantford, Ont., 92 Dufferin Street.
Deadman, William James, Beeton, Ont.
Fraser, Donald Thomas, York Mills, Ont.
Gillrie, Frederick Russell, Hamilton, Ont., 255 King St. W.
Gorman, Morley Edward, Oakville, R. R. No. 1.
Hamilton, Harold Parrish, Uxbridge, Ont.

Helliwell, Maurice Round, Toronto, 525 Confederation Life Building.
Hodge, William Roy, London, Ont., 304 Wolfe St.
Howitt, John Ransom, Hamilton, Ont., 104 George St.
Hutton, William Lorne, Brantford, Ont., 221 Nelson St.
Jeffrey, Edward Shapter, Toronto, Ont., 107 Carlton St.
Keillor, Clifford M., Wallacetown, Ont.
Kirkham, Frederick Russell, Toronto, 640 Bathurst St.
Martin, Herbert Carl, Hamilton, Ont., 132 Hughson St. N.
Martin, Robert Beattie, London, Ont., 268 Ridout St.
Moon, Athol Alexander, Cottam, Ont.
McQuay, Robert Whiteman, Foxwarren, Man.
O'Sullivan, Paul Michael, Toronto, 1155 King Street W.
Overend, Samuel Alexander, Caledonia, Ont.
Paul, Reginald, Sebringville, Ont.
Scott, David Emerson, Spry, Ont.
Smith, Harry Roy, Toronto, Ont., 48 Yorkville Ave.
Storms, Thomas Harold Douglas, Hamilton, Ont., 53 Bay St. S.
Van Wyck, Hermon Brookfield, Chatham, Ont.
Walsh, Stanley Young, Peterboro, Ont., 317 Margaret Ave.
Wishart, David Edmund, Toronto, Ont., 45 Grosvenor St.
Whytock, Harry Wishart, Madoc, Ontario.
All of which is respectfully submitted.

H. S. GRIFFIN,
President.

Dr. King read the Legislative Committee's report re Reciprocity with Great Britain and, after a short discussion, on motion by Dr. Jarvis, seconded by Dr. Hamilton, the Council went into Committee of the Whole on the report, with Dr. Addison in the chair, when the same was considered clause by clause, and on request Dr. King read all the correspondence in connection with the necessary negotiations which had been carried on.

On motion of Dr. Ryan, seconded by Dr. Arthur, the committee rose and reported progress.

The President, Dr. Griffin, resumed the chair, when, on motion of Dr. Hardy, the Council adjourned to meet at 10 a.m. Thursday, July 1st, 1915. (Approved).

H. S. GRIFFIN,
President.

THIRD DAY

MORNING SESSION.

Thursday, July 1st, 1915.

The Council met at ten o'clock a.m. in accordance with the motion for adjournment.

The President took the chair and called the Council to order.

The Secretary called the Roll and the following members answered to their names: Drs. Addison, Arthur, Argue, Becker, Brodie, Crain, Cruickshank, Dales, Emmerson, Farncomb, Ferguson, Sir James Grant, Drs. Griffin, Hamilton, Hardy, Jarvis, Johnson, Kellam, King, J. MacCallum, S. McCallum, Routledge, Ryan, Spankie, Stewart, Walters, Wickens.

The Secretary read the minutes of the last session, which were confirmed and signed by the President.

COMMUNICATIONS, PETITIONS, ETC.

The Secretary read communication re College of Mano-Therapy, Hamilton, which was referred to Education Committee.

RECEPTION OF REPORTS OF COMMITTEES.

Dr. Emmerson presented the report of the Rules and Regulations Committee re by-laws.

Dr. Spankie presented the report of the representatives to the Medical Council of Canada.

Dr. J. MacCallum presented the report of special committee re Registrar.

Dr. Wickens presented the report of the Education Committee.

NOTICES OF MOTION.

Dr. Dales gave notice that he would move, seconded by Dr. Hamilton, that this Council should have a proper register of its members, and that the printing committee be instructed to proceed to prepare said Register; and in it, the men who have failed to pay their annual fees be placed in a separate list, with the amount of arrearages.

Dr. Cruickshank gave notice, seconded by Dr. Hamilton, that he would move that the Legislative Committee be instructed to secure evidence to be presented to the probable Medical Commission of the Ontario Government.

Motions of which Notice Has Been Given at a Previous Session.

It is moved by Dr. Brodie, seconded by Dr. Dales, that the Legislative Committee secure an amendment to the Public Health Act, as follows: In all cases of death, where the deceased had been attended by an unlicensed practitioner, it shall be the duty of the regular physician, if the death takes place within ten days of said attendance, to report said death to the Coroner for investigation.

It was moved in amendment by Dr. Ferguson, seconded by Dr. Cruickshank, that the motion by Dr. Brodie be referred to the Legislative Committee.

The President put the amendment which, on a vote having been taken, was declared carried.

Enquiries.

Dr. Cruickshank made the following enquiries:

(1) When will the Commission of Medical Practice be appointed by the Ontario Government?

(2) What will be the character of the Commission?

(3) What procedure will it follow?

(4) What steps are being taken to procure evidence for the same?

The above enquiries were answered by the President and Dr. King.

Consideration of Reports.

Dr. Spankie read the report of representatives on Medical Council of Canada and moved, seconded by Dr. Ryan, that the same be adopted.

Before its adoption, at the request of Dr. Spankie, Dr. Gibson, President of the Dominion Medical Council, addressed the members, giving information as to the work of the Dominion Council.

The President then put the motion to adopt the report, which, on a vote having been taken, was declared carried and the report adopted as follows:

Report of Representatives on Medical Council of Canada.

To the President and Members of the Council of the College of Physicians and Surgeons of Ontario:

Gentlemen:—The third annual meeting of the Medical Council of Canada was held in the City of Ottawa on the 8th and 9th of June, 1915, and the regular business was proceeded with in the usual way.

Since our last report examinations were held at Montreal in October, 1914, and at Winnipeg, in June, 1915, with the following results: At the October examination 86 tried, 49 passed, 22 failed, 15 were referred. At the June examination this year 40 tried, 21 passed, 12 failed and 7 were referred.

The examinations will be held at Montreal and St. John in October this year, and in Toronto and Winnipeg in June, 1916.

We hand herewith a complete copy of the minutes of the meeting and beg to call your attention to the following chief features :

1. Very few practitioners are seeking registration under the ten year clause, only 133 up to the end of financial year, 31st March, and this number includes the members of the Council.

2. An effort is being made to secure uniform standards of Medical Education in the various Provinces and to this end a Committee is constituted and a copy of their first report will be found in the minutes. In this connection it is to be noted that the Canadian Medical Association has appointed a committee to report on the question of uniformity in Provincial Medical Legislation.

3. On applications for registration without examination on account of Canadian Expeditionary Forces the Council adopted the report of its Executive Committee, stating that it is inexpedient at this time to grant to any applicant the license of the Dominion Medical Council wihout examination.

4. The Medical Council of Canada placed itself on record as favorable to reciprocity in Medical Licensure with the General Medical Council of the United Kingdom, and urges that the various Provinces do all in their power to hasten the attainment of this issue.

The following are the officers of the Medical Council of Canada for the ensuing year.

Honorary President—Sir T. G. Roddick.

President, Dr. R. J. Gibson.

Vice-President—Dr. J. Stewart.

Registrar—Dr. R. W. Powell.

All of which is respectfully submitted.

W. S. SPANKIE.
R. J. GIBSON.

(For complete copy of the minutes of the annual meeting of the Medical Council of Canada, held at Ottawa, June 8th, 1915, and referred to in the preceding report, see minute-book of Ontario Medical Council).

Dr. J. MacCallum read the report of the special committee re Registrar and moved, seconded by Dr. Ferguson, that the report be adopted.

Dr. H. J. Hamilton moved in amendment, seconded by Dr. Dales, that the report be referred back to the committee with the object of amending the report so that the same person shall not be named as Registrar and Treasurer.

The President put the amendment, which on a vote having been taken was declared lost.

Dr. J. MacCallum then re-moved, seconded by Dr. Ferguson, the adoption of the report as read, and that clause two be referred to the Finance Committee.

The President put the motion, which, on a vote having been taken, was declared carried and the report adopted, as follows:

REPORT OF SPECIAL COMMITTEE RE REGISTRAR.

To the President and Members of the College of Physicians and Surgeons of Ontario:

Gentlemen:—Your committee to whom was referred the letter and resignation of Dr. J. L. Bray, Registrar, beg leave to report as follows:

1.   That the resignation of Dr. Bray as Registrar be accepted.

2.   That the Finance Committee be requested to make a suitable retiring allowance to Dr. Bray.

3.   That Dr. H. W. Aikins, Treasurer, be appointed Registrar and Treasurer at a salary of $2,000 per annuam for the combined duties of Registrar and Treasurer.

All of which is respectfully submitted.

JAMES MacCallum,
Chairman.

Dr. Emmerson read the reports of the Discipline Committee: (1) Dr. William Macdonald Adams, (2) re Harry Alfred Turofsky, (3) Re Dr. Walker's Institute.

Dr. Emmerson moved, seconded by Dr. Hardy, that clause one of the report re Dr. Adams be adopted.

The President put the motion, which, on a vote having been taken, was declared carried.

Dr. Emmerson moved, seconded by Dr. Hardy, that clause two of the report re Dr. Turofsky be adopted.

The President put the motion which, on a vote having been taken, was declared adopted.

Dr. Emmerson moved, seconded by Dr. Hardy, that clause three of the report re Dr. Walker be adopted.

After discussion it was moved in amendment by Dr. Wickens, seconded by Dr. Hardy, that the consideration of that part of the report of the Discipline Committee dealing with the cause of Dr. Walker be postponed till a further session of the Council.

The President put the motion, which, on a vote having been taken, was declared carried.

The reports of the Discipline Committee re Dr. Adams and Dr. Turofsky are as follows:

RE WILLIAM MACDONALD ADAMS.
REPORT.

At a meeting of the Discipline Committee duly called and held on Wednesday, the third day of February, 1915, charges against William Macdonald Adams, of which due notice had been given, were considered by the Committee, all the members of the Committee being present, as follows:

Drs. T. W. H. Young (Chairman), W. E. Crain, A. E. Wickens, A. T. Emmerson.

Dr. Adams was present in person.

The charge against Dr. Adams was for selling opium and morphine to one Charles Anderson.

After hearing the evidence, including the evidence of Dr. Adams explaining his conduct in the matter, the Committee were of opinion that Dr. Adams was indiscreet in selling the drug in the manner in which he did sell it and failing to keep a proper record of such sale, but under all the circumstances, having regard to the fact that only a single sale was proved, the committee are of the opinion that Dr. Adams ought not to be found guilty of infamous or disgraceful conduct in a professional respect, but that he should be reprimanded for his conduct in connection with the said sale, and the committee so report.

A. T. EMMERSON,
Acting Chairman.

RE HARRY ALFRED TUROFSKY.
REPORT.

At a meeting of the Discipline Committee duly called and held on Wednesday, the third day of February, 1915, charges against Harry Alfred Turofsky, of which due notice had been given, were considered by the Committee, all the members of the Committee being present, as follows:

Drs. T. W. H. Young (Chairman), A. E. Wickens, W. E. Crain, A. T. Emmerson.

Dr. Turofsky was present in person and was also represented by Counsel.

A number of witnesses were called, after which Dr. Turofsky's evidence and explanations were given.

After full consideration of the matter the Committee unanimously decided to find Dr. Turofsky not guilty of the charges made, and therefore so report.

A. T. EMMERSON,
Acting Chairman.

On motion of Dr. Jarvis, Council adjourned to meet at 2 p.m., July 1st, 1915.

H. S. GRIFFIN,
President.

The Council met at two o'clock p.m. in accordance with the motion for adjournment.

The President took the Chair and called the Council to order.

The Registrar called the Roll and the following members answered to their names: Drs. Addison, Brodie, Cruickshank, Dales, Emmerson, Farncomb, Griffin, Hamilton, Kellam, J. MacCallum, S. McCallum, Routledge, Ryan, Spankie.

Shortly afterwards the following members took their seats: Drs. Argue, Becker, Crain, Ferguson, Sir James Grant, Drs. Hardy, Jarvis, Johnson, King, Stewart, Walters, Wickens.

The minutes of the morning session were read and adopted.

RECEPTION OF REPORTS OF COMMITTEES.

Dr. Ferguson presented the report of the Education Committee.

NOTICES OF MOTION.

(1) Dr. King gave notice that he would move at the next meeting, seconded by Dr. Stewart, that a sum not to exceed $500

be placed at the disposal of the Executive Committee for the purpose of conducting an investigation into the methods, schools, appliances and so forth of the Osteopathic, Chiropractic or other practic schools, and that they be instructed to gain as much evidence as possible before the next meeting of the Council.

(2) Dr. Argue gave notice that he would move, seconded by Dr. Farncomb, that the Printing Committee be instructed to make the Medical Register as complete as possible, and that the Registrar be instructed to send each territorial representative a list of the members in his division for the purpose of having it corrected as far as possible.

(3) Sir James Grant gave notice that he would move, seconded by Dr. E. E. King, that the attention of the Prime Minister of Ontario be invited to the desirability of the district medical inspectors of Ontario delivering in each district a few public lectures on the sanitation of the farm, with the prospect of correcting any defects in sanitation and thus guarding the infant life, particularly of Ontario, and that Dr. King, Dr. Johnson, Dr. Hardy and the Secretary be empowered to interview the Hon. Mr. Hearst with that object in view.

(4) Dr. Argue gave notice that he would move, seconded by Dr. Crain, that Dr. Harold Courtenay be granted his license on account of going on Overseas Service.

(5) Dr. Stewart gave notice, seconded by Dr. Spankie, that he would move that Miss Rose be granted an honorarium of one hundred and fifty dollars for her valuable services to this Council during the past year, in addition to her regular salary.

MOTIONS OF WHICH NOTICE HAS BEEN GIVEN AT A PREVIOUS SESSION.

Dr. F. A. Dales moved, seconded by Dr. Hamilton, the following motion of which notice was given at an earlier session. That this Council should have a proper Register of its members, and that the printing committee be instructed to proceed to prepare such register; and, in it, the men who have failed to pay their annual fee be placed in a separate list with amount of arrearages.

The President put the motion, which, on a vote having been taken, was declared lost.

Dr. Cruickshank moved, seconded by Dr. Hamilton, the following motion, of which notice was given at an earlier session: That the legislative committee be instructed to secure evidence to be presented to the probable medical commission of the Ontario Government.

The President put the motion, which on a vote having been taken, was declared carried.

Consideration of Reports.

Dr. Ryan read the report of the Complaints Committee, and moved, seconded by Dr. Ferguson, that the report be adopted.

The President put the motion, which, on a vote having been taken, was declared carried, and the report adopted as follows:

Report of the Complaints Committee.

To the President and Members of the Council of the College of Physicians and Surgeons of Ontario:

Gentlemen:—Your Committee on Complaints beg leave to report their decision on the following Appeals to the recent examination:

Howard Black ....Appeal Granted.
R. A. Bond ....Appeal Granted.
C. M. Burroughs ....Appeal Not Granted.
R. M. Cairns ....Appeal Not Granted.
H. D. Courtenay ....Appeal Not Granted.
L. C. Fallis ....Appeal Not Granted.
E. Gardiner ....Appeal Not Granted.
S. Golber ....Appeal Not Granted.
W. C. Hancy ....Appeal Granted.
D. E. Lang ....Appeal Not Granted.
A. G. Ley ....Appeal Not Granted.
G. C. Livingstone ....Appeal Granted.
H. C. McCaul ....Appeal Not Granted.
W. M. MacKay ....Appeal Not Granted.
Herbert W. Martin ....Appeal Not Granted.
W. G. Martin ....Appeal Not Granted.
D. Rigg ....Appeal Granted.
J. A. Stewart ....Appeal Not Granted.
W. L. Tyrer ....Appeal Not Granted.
H. C. Allison ....Appeal Granted.
W. L. Yule ....Appeal Not Granted.
O. J. S. Little ....Appeal Not Granted.
R. B. Richardson ....Appeal Granted.

All of which is respectfully submitted.

EDWARD RYAN,
Chairman.

Dr. Ferguson read the report of the Education Committee and moved, seconded by Dr. Wickens, that the report be adopted.

The President put the motion, which, on a vote having been taken, was declared carried, and the report adopted as follows:

Report of Education Committee.

To the President and Members of the Council of the College of Physicians and Surgeons of Ontario:

Gentlemen:—

1. Your Committee recommends that a Committee consisting of Drs. Ferguson, Addison and Wickens be appointed to correspond with the Registrars of the various Provinces with a view of obtaining a uniform standard of Matriculation for all Provinces. Committee to report at next session of Council.

2. In re the question of allotting a definite number of hours to each subject in the Curriculum instead of the rather indefinite wording of the present regulations in Section 2, Sub-section 3.

Your Committee recommends that a Committee composed of Drs. Ferguson, Ryan and J. MacCallum be appointed to look into the details of the proposed changes and report at the next session of the Council.

3. A communication was received from the Registrar-Treasurer of the College of Pharmacy calling attention to Section 27 of the Pharmacy Act in regard to the endorsation by this Council of the revised British Pharmacopoeia for use by the physicians of this Province.

Your Committee recommends that the letter, together with the copy of the Pharmacy Act, be filed with the Registrar, and that the Council go on record as endorsing the revised British Pharmacopoeia, and advise dispensing according to its formula, dating from September 1st, 1915.

4. A communication from A. T. Colville, Hamilton, through his solicitors, asking the Council to endorse his "Canadian College of Mano-Therapy" was considered.

Your Committee does not consider it advisable to endorse any undertakings of Mr. Colville, who has been repeatedly and successfully prosecuted for practising illegally.

5. Re the appointment of Examiners:—

The Committee recommend that the following examiners be appointed.

Board of Examiners, 1915-1916.

Dr. Edwin Seaborn, London, Ont.—Surgery.
Dr. Peter Stuart, Guelph, Ont.—Surgery.
Dr. W. T. Connell, Kingston, Ont.—Medicine.
Dr. J. P. Vrooman, Napanee, Ont.—Medicine.
Dr. F. A. Cleland, Toronto, Ont.—Midwifery and Diseases of Women.

Dr. W. A. Thomson, London, Ont.—Midwifery and Diseases of Women.

Dr. W. A. McFall, Toronto, Ont.—Homoeopathic Examiner.

Dr. G. L. Husband, Hamilton, Ont.—Homoeopathic Examiner.

All of which is respectfully submitted.

R. FERGUSON,

Chairman.

Dr. King moved, seconded by Dr. Ryan, that the report of the Legislative Committee on reciprocity with Great Britain be adopted.

The President put the motion, which, on a vote having been taken, was declared carried.

The report is as follows:

THE COLLEGE OF PHYSICIANS AND SURGEONS OF ONTARIO,
LEGISLATION COMMITTEE.

That this Committee report to the Council of the College of Physicians and Surgeons of Ontario at the next meeting thereof, to be held on the 29th day of June, 1915, as follows:

1. That at a special meeting of the Council of the said College, held on the 22nd of December, 1914, the following resolution was passed:

That all preliminary arrangements necessary to bring into force the British Reciprocity be referred to the Legislation Committee and that the subject be referred to the Solicitor of the College for advice as to the necessity of securing the passage of an Enabling Clause; and to enter into negotiations with the Council of Great Britain on terms to enable this reciprocity to become effective and report to the next regular meeting of the Council.

2. That pursuant to the said resolution the subject of reciprocity with Great Britain was referred for advice to the solicitor, who advised that an application be made for an amendment to the Ontario Medical Act for the purpose of removing all doubts as to the power of the Council to make the necessary arrangements for reciprocal registration in Ontario and Great Britain upon identical terms and conditions.

3. That the matter was duly laid before the Government of the Province of Ontario, with the result that the Ontario Medical Amendment Act of 1915, of which copy accompanies this report, was duly passed.

4. That the correspondence accompanying this report has passed between the Registrar of the College and the Registrar of the General Medical Council of Great Britain.

5. That this committee, being of opinion that reciprocity with Great Britain should be made effective at the earliest possible date, instructed the solicitor to prepare the necessary Regulation* which accompanies this report, and which the committee now recommends for adoption by the Council.

6. That this committee, being of opinion that it is desirable to avoid any difficulty or misunderstanding, directed the Registrar to forward to the Registrar of the General Medical Council a copy of the said proposed regulation with a request that any objection be communicated by letter or cable on or before June 29th, the date of the meeting of the Council.

EDMUND E. KING,
Chairman.

*REGULATION.

Every Medical Practitioner registered in the Medical Register of the United Kingdom of Great Britain and Ireland, upon proof to the satisfaction of the Registrar of the College of Physicians and Surgeons of Ontario, that he is so registered, and that he is of good character, and that he is by law entitled to practice medicine, surgery and midwifery in the United Kingdom, shall, on application to the said Registrar, and on payment of such fee, not exceeding One hundred Dollars, as shall be the fee, which, by Regulation of the Council, shall be from time to time charged for registration of all persons entitled to be registered in the Province of Ontario, be entitled, without examination in the Province of Ontario, to be registered under the provisions of the Ontario Medical Act.

Provided that he proves to the satisfaction of the Registrar the following circumstance:

That the diploma or diplomas, in respect of which he was registered in the said Medical Register of the United Kingdom, was or were granted to him, at a time when he was not domiciled in the Province of Ontario, or in the course of a period of not less than five years, during the whole of which he resided out of the Province of Ontario.

The documents which accompanied the report above and which are voluminous, may be inspected by reference to the files at the College Building. They are as follows:

1. Regulation.

2. Certified copy of Ontario Medical Amendment Act, 1915.

3. Forms of application by British Medical Practitioners.

4. Forms in use in England.

5. Correspondence with the Registrar of the General Medical Council, London.

6. Draft letter to be written by the Registrar after the regulation has been passed.

7. Letters from the solicitor to the Chairmen of the Legislation Committee.

By permission of the Council, the report of the Registration Committee was presented.

The report of the Finance Committee was also presented by Dr. J. MacCallum, who moved, seconded by Dr. Hamilton, that the report of the Finance Committee be adopted.

It was moved in amendment by Dr. King, seconded by Dr. Emmerson, that· $2,000 be substituted for one thousand in the contribution to the Belgian Relief Fund.

The President put the amendment, which, on a vote having been taken, was declared carried.

It was moved in amendment by Dr. A. T. Emmerson, seconded by Dr. Addison, that the sessional allowance be ten dollars for each half day in session and ten dollars for each half day in travelling, with five cents per mile each way.

The President put the amendment which, on a vote having been taken, was declared lost.

The President then put the motion to adopt the report of the Finance Committee, as amended, which, on a vote having been taken, was declared carried and the report adopted as follows:

REPORT OF FINANCE COMMITTEE.

To the Members of the Council of the College of Physicians and Surgeons of Ontario.

Your committee beg leave to report to Council that we have examined the Treasurer's report, properly audited and find a balance in bank, June 16th, 1915, of $24,308.77.

We recommend that the Council subscribe the sum of one thousand dollars to the Relief Fund of Belgian Physicians and Pharmacists.

We recommend that Dr. W. R. Campbell be paid $10 for textbooks borrowed by examiners and lost.

We recommend that the request of William Matthew Wallace for refund of twenty-five dollars paid as matriculation fee for son who died before examination, be granted.

.We recommend that request of Dr. J. T. Bowman, London, for refund be not entertained, and that similar requests from Dr. McDiarmid of Ingersoll and Dr. D. E. Bell, Kingston, be not entertained.

Owing to the fact that Dr. T. H. W. Young, of Peterboro, member of the Council for District No. 14 is absent on active service, your committee recommend that his sessional indemnity be paid.

We recommend that an honorarium of $750 be granted the late Registrar, Dr. Bray.

We recommend that the sessional indemnity be the same as last year.

We recommend that all appeals for reconsideration of examination papers must be made before the next ensuing meeting of this Council.

Your committee also recommend that a fee of $5 be charged all applicants making appeals for reconsideration of their examination papers of this Council in future, which fee will be refunded to each of those applicants whose appeal is granted.

We recommend that Drs. Johnson or Hamilton and the Registrar be empowered to open the safety deposit box in the vault of the National Trust Company on behalf of this Council.

All of which is respectfully submitted.

JAMES MACCALLUM,
Chairman.

Dr. Cruickshank moved, seconded by Dr. Hamilton, that the report of the Registration Committee be adopted.

The President put the motion, which, on a vote having been taken, was declared carried and the report adopted as follows:

Report of the Régistration Committee.

To the President and Members of the Council of the College of Physicians and Surgeons of Ontario:

Gentlemen:—Your Committee on Registration begs to report as follows:

Re communication of Lt. Col. Marlow referring to graduates of 1915, who are Army Medical Corps officers desiring special consideration, we recommend that each case be considered on its merits.

Re C. B. Williams who has gone to the Front and has matriculated at Toronto University, the Committee would recommend his registration as a Matriculant be granted.

Re Dr. J. C. Connell's letter. No Matriculation can be considered without some evidence of knowledge of Latin. Candidate can comply by passing examination in Latin.

Re Dr. G. G. Membery who failed in several subjects of the Council Examination, and who is registered in Great Britain and who is now at the Front. No provision is yet provided for Reciprocity with Great Britain, but it is expected to be realized soon.

Re George F. Seaborn. Request granted.

Re T. R. Bailey. Request granted.

Re Adam Ardiel. Matriculation accepted and to be admitted to Final Examination.

Re Thomas A. Winslow. Would refer him to Sec. 6, Subsection 2, which requires attendance of at least one session in an Ontario College.

Re Charles F. Fenwick: That he be granted registration as a Matriculant.

Re L. B. Lyon: That Matriculation be granted.

Re W. S. Patrick: That Matriculation be granted.

Re W. M. McLaren: He has no standing in the College of Physicians and Surgeons of Ontario.

Re G. W. MacNeil. That Matriculation be granted.

Re R. B. Richardson: That he be allowed registration as a Matriculant.

Re the application of F. X. O'Connor, M.D., serving with the Canadian Expeditionary Forces, for License, be granted.

Re Registration of Dr. M. G. Thomson, that his Matriculation be granted.

All of which is respectfully submitted.

(Sgd.) G. R. CRUICKSHANK,
Chairman.

Dr. Emmerson moved, seconded by Dr. Ferguson, that the Discipline Committee's report re Dr. Charles William Walker be adopted.

On the yeas and nays being taken the report was declared adopted, the yeas and nays resulting as follows:

Yeas: Drs. Addison, Argue, Becker, Brodie, Crain, Cruickshank, Dales, Emmerson, Farncomb, Ferguson, Sir James Grant, Griffin, Hamilton, Hardy, Jarvis, King, J. MacCallum, Routledge, Walters, Wickens—twenty yeas.

Nays: (None).

The report as adopted is as follows:

DISCIPLINE COMMITTEE REPORT.
RE CHARLES WILLIAM WALKER.

At a meeting of the Discipline Committee, duly called and held on Wednesday, the third day of February, 1915, charges against Charles William Walker, of which due notice had been given, were considered by the Committee, all the members of the Committee being present, as follows: Drs. T. W. H. Young (Chairman), A. E. Wickens, W. E. Crain, A. T. Emmerson.

Dr. Walker was present in person and was also represented by Counsel.

The committee have ascertained and report to the Council the following facts:

1. That the charges made against the said Charles William Walker are set forth in the notice served upon him attached to this report and marked Exhibit "A."

2. That the evidence taken in support of the said charges, including the evidence of the said Charles William Walker, is contained in the shorthand report of the proceedings before the committee attached to this report, and marked Exhibit "B."

3. That the said Charles William Walker did in fact manage and conduct the Ontario Medical Institute, or Dr. Walker's Ontario Medical Institute as charged, and did employ therein and in connection therewith unregistered assistants as charged.

4. That the said Charles William Walker did, in connection with the said institute or institutes, publish the advertisements hereunto attached and marked Exhibit "C."

5. That the said Charles William Walker in conducting the said institute or institutes in the manner stated in the evidence and advertising the same as proved, was in the opinion of the Committee guilty of infamous and disgraceful conduct in a professional respect, and the Committee recommend to the Council that action be taken in the premises by erasing the name of the said Charles William Walker from the Register.

A. T. EMMERSON,
(Acting) Chairman.

(For Exhibits A, B and C referred to in the foregoing report see files of the College).

It was moved by Dr. Emmerson, seconded by Dr. Ferguson, that the Discipline Committee's report re Dr. H. E. Sheppard, be adopted.

The President put the motion, which, on a vote having been taken, was declared carried and the report adopted as follows:

REPORT OF DISCIPLINE COMMITTEE.
July 1st, 1915.

In the matter of Dr. Sheppard who applies to have his name placed on our Register, and which has been referred to your committee, we recommend that no action be taken, as at a previous meeting the matter was before the Council, and it was decided to allow him to be reinstated so soon as he pays the amount he is indebted to the Council in.

A. T. EMMERSON.

Dr. Emmerson presented the report of the Rules and Regulations Committee, re by-laws, Nos. 1 to 14.

On motion of Dr. Emmerson, seconded by Dr. Ferguson, the Council went into Committee of the Whole on the by-laws, with Dr. Argue in the chair.

The by-laws were considered one by one in Committee of the Whole and, as amended, were adopted.

On motion of Dr. Emmerson, seconded by Dr. Ferguson, the committee rose, the President resumed the chair, when Dr. Emmerson reported the by-laws, as amended, adopted in Committee of the Whole.

Dr. Emmerson then moved, seconded by Dr. Ferguson, that the by-laws as amended, be now read a third time, adopted in Council, signed by the President, and sealed with the Seal of the College.

The President put the motion, which, on a vote having been taken, was declared carried.

(For by-laws Nos. 1 to 14 see first part of Announcement).

By consent of the Council Dr. Johnson presented and read the report of the Property Committee.

Dr. Johnson then moved, seconded by Dr. Stewart, that the report of the Property Committee be adopted.

The President put the motion, which, on a vote having been taken, was declared carried.

Dr. Johnson asked permission to modify the wording of the report, to be brought in, as so modified, at the morning session next following. (Permission given).

By permission of the Council notices of motion were given by Dr. Argue, re Medical Register; by Sir James Grant, re sanitation of the farm; by Dr. Argue re applicant Courtenay; and by Dr. Stewart, re honorarium to Miss Rose.

On motion of Dr. Ryan, seconded by Dr. Spankie, the Council then adjourned until ten o'clock, Friday morning, July 2nd, 1915.

(Minutes confirmed July 2nd, 1915).

H. S. GRIFFIN,
President.

FOURTH DAY

MORNING SESSION.

Friday, July 2nd, 1915.

The Council met at ten o'clock a.m. in accordance with the motion for adjournment.

The President took the chair and called the Council to order.

The Registrar called the Roll and the following members answered to their names: Drs. Arthur, Argue, Becker, Brodie, Crain, Cruickshank, Dales, Emmerson, Farncomb, Ferguson, Griffin, Hamilton, Hardy, Jarvis, King, Routledge, Ryan, Spankie, Stewart, Walters, Wickens.

Shortly afterwards the following members took their seats. Drs. Addison, Sir James Grant, Drs. Johnson, Kellam, J. MacCallum.

The minutes of the last session were read and confirmed.

Dr. Johnson presented the report of the Prosecutions Committee, which was received.

NOTICES OF MOTION.

Dr. E. E. King, gave notice that he would move, seconded by Dr. Stewart, that it be an instruction to the Registrar to prepare a circular letter, setting out the fact that a register exists, that an annual fee is payable to the College, that unless change of address is forwarded to the College, disadvantages to the licentiates may accrue, that to ensure his franchise the correctness of the register is essential, and any other information that a recent licentiate should know.

MOTIONS OF WHICH NOTICE HAS BEEN GIVEN AT A PREVIOUS SESSION.

Dr. E. E. King moved, seconded by Dr. Stewart, the following motion, of which notice was given at an earlier session: That a sum not to exceed five hundred dollars be placed at the disposal of the Executive Committee for the purpose of conducting an investigation into the method, schools, appliances, and so forth of the Osteopathic, Chiropractic or other practic schools, and that they be instructed to gain as much evidence as possible before the next meeting of the Council.

It was moved in amendment by Dr. J. MacCallum, seconded by Dr. Cruickshank, that the motion be amended to read that a sum not to exceed one thousand dollars be substituted for the words "five hundred dollars."

The President put the amendment which, on a vote having been taken, was declared carried.

The President then put the motion, as amended, which, on a vote having been taken, was declared carried.

Dr. Argue moved, seconded by Dr. Farncomb, the following motion of which notice was given at an earlier session: That the printing committee be instructed to make the medical register as complete as possible and that the Registrar be instructed to send each territorial representative a list of the members in his division for the purpose of having it corrected as far as possible.

The President put the motion, which, on a vote having been taken, was declared carried.

Sir James Grant moved, seconded by Dr. E. E. King, the following motion of which notice was given at an earlier session:

That the attention of the Prime Minister of Ontario be invited to the desirability of the district medical inspectors of Ontario delivering in each district a few public lectures on the Sanitation of the Farm with the prospect of correcting any defects in sanitation and thus guarding the infant life, particularly of Ontario, and that Dr. King, Dr. Johnson, Dr. Hardy and the Secretary be empowered to interview the Hon. Mr. Hearst with that object in view.

The President put the motion which, on a vote having been taken, was declared carried.

Dr. Argue moved, seconded by Dr. Crain, the following motion, of which notice was given at an earlier session.

That Dr. Harold Courtenay be granted his license on account of going on Overseas Service.

The President put the motion, which, on a vote having been taken, was declared lost.

Dr. Stewart moved, seconded by Dr. Spankie, the following motion, of which notice was given at an earlier session:

That Miss Rose be granted an honorarium of $150 for her valuable services to this Council during the past year, in addition to her regular salary.

The President put the motion, which, on a vote having been taken, was declared carried.

CONSIDERATION OF REPORTS.

It was moved by Dr. Johnson, seconded by Dr. Stewart, that the report of the Property Committee, as amended, be adopted.

The President put the motion, which, on a vote having been taken, was declared carried, and the report adopted as follows:

Toronto, Ont., July 2nd, 1915.

To the President and Members of the College of Physicians and Surgeons of Ontario:

Gentlemen:—I have the honor to present the report of the Property Committee of the Council.

In accordance with the resolution passed by this Council last December, your Committee have carried out the instructions therein contained, viz., a vault has been built and equipped, and a limited amount of electric wiring and fixtures have been installed.

The building and grounds are in a fairly good state of repair and have been carefully looked after, but the building requires painting and papering and otherwise cleaning up.. A new walk must be laid down from the street line to the front of this building, and arrangements made by which an entrance to the rear of our property can be obtained if necessary.

The furniture is in a good state of repair.

All of which is respectfully submitted.

(Sgd.) ARTHUR JUKES JOHNSON,
Chairman.

Dr. Johnson presented the report of the Printing Committee. re printing Annual Announcement and moved, seconded by Dr. King that the report be adopted.

The President put the motion, which, on a vote having been taken, was declared carried and the report adopted as follows:

Toronto, July 2nd, 1915.

To the President and Members of the College of Physicians and Surgeons of Ontario:

Gentlemen.—I have the honor to report that your Committee on Printing met and organized;

That a communication has been received from the printer who printed the last Annual Announcement, offering to undertake the work again at a slightly lower cost.

All of which is respectfully submitted.

ARTHUR JUKES JOHNSON,
Chairman.

Dr. Johnson moved, seconded by Dr. Kellam, that the report of the Prosecutions Committee, to which is attached the Prosecutor's annual report, be adopted.

The President put the motion, which, on a vote having been taken, was declared carried and the report adopted as follows:

To the President and Members of the College of Physicians and Surgeons of Ontario:

Gentlemen:—I have the honor to present the report of the Prosecuting Committee of this Council. Your committee has met from time to time as necessity arose, and has considered the cases brought to their notice by the Prosecutor, whose report is hereto attached.

All of which is respectfully submitted.

ARTHUR JUKES JOHNSON,
Chairman.

Toronto, June 1st, 1915.

To the Chairman and Members of the Prosecution Committee of the Ontario Medical Council:

Gentlemen:—I beg leave to submit my Annual Report re Prosecutions and Investigations.

NAME.	ADDRESS.	DISPOSITION OF CASE.
Georges Dupont	Ottawa	Fined $25.00 or 30 days in Gaol. Fine paid.
John Roach	Brechin	Fined $25.00 or 30 days in Gaol. Fine paid.
John McLean	Orillia	Fined $25.00 or 30 days in Gaol. Fine paid.
James Richardson	Noelville	Fined $25.00 or 30 days in Gaol. Fine paid.
Adrien Bonin	Bonfield	Fined $25.00 or 30 days in Gaol. Fine paid.
Julius Weichels	Stratford	Fined $50.00 or 60 days in Gaol. He appealed to County Judge. Appeal dismissed. Fine paid.
A. T. Colville	Mitchell	Fined $50.00 or 30 days in Gaol. Fine paid.
C. C. Cornish	Ingersoll	Charge withdrawn.
Lapenta	Hamilton	Left country before he could be served.
J. L. White	St. Catharines	Fined $25.00 or 30 days in Gaol.
Elizabeth A. Lumb	Runnymede	Fined $25.00 or 30 days in Gaol. Fine paid.
Rebecca Caplin	Toronto	Case dismissed.
Dabey Close	Toronto	Case dismissed.
Elizabeth Henn	Toronto	Fined $25.00 or 30 days in Gaol. Fine paid.
J. Ward	Toronto	Fined $25.00 or 30 days in Gaol. Fine paid.
L. G. Hodder	White River	Fined $25.00 or 30 days in Gaol. Fine paid.
W. S. Hodgins	Fort William	Fined $40.00 or 30 days in Gaol. Fine paid.
J. E. Merritt	Huntsville	Fined $30.00 or 30 days in Gaol. Fine paid.
C. H. Granger	Toronto	Fined $25.00 or 30 days in Gaol. Fine paid.
J. W. Black	Toronto	Fined $25.00 or 30 days in Gaol. Fine paid.

John Roach ....Brechin ....Fined \$25.00 or 30 days in
Gaol. Appeal to Division Court pending.

Angelina Curto ....Hamilton ....Fined \$25.00 or 30 days in
Gaol. Fine paid.

Angelina Curto ....Hamilton ....Withdrawn defendant paying costs.

Joseph MacDonald....Delhi ....Fined \$25.00 or 30 days in
Gaol. Fine paid.

RECAPITULATION.

Informations laid	24
Convictions	19
Cases dismissed	2
Left country before he could be served	1
Charge withdrawn	2
Total	24

There were a number of complaints about Osteopaths, Chiropractors, Christian Scientists, and one in which a man, who a short time ago was an hostler at a hotel, now advertises by card that he cures all kinds of disease, without the use of knife or medicine. These cases were all enquired into, and reported on.

I beg leave to report that the names of Dr. H. A. Turofsky, 185 Spadina Ave., Toronto, Dr. W. M. Adams, 267 Queen St. W., Toronto, and Dr. C. W. Walker, 263 Yonge St., Toronto, were sent on by the Council at their last meeting, to the Discipline Committee, to investigate a charge of infamous and disgraceful conduct in a professional sense, against each of them, and you will have the report of said Committee on each case laid before you.

I have also to report that Dr. C. K. Robinson, of Tamworth, Ontario, was tried before the Criminal Court, at Napanee, on a criminal charge in connection with the death of a woman during an operation, but was acquitted. It will be for the Council to decide whether his name should go to the Discipline Committee for investigation or otherwise.

In conclusion, I beg leave to thank you and also the majority of the Profession for the assistance given me in the discharge of my duties.

Your obedient servant,

JOHN FYFE,
Prosecutor.

Receipts for 1914 and 1915.

DATE.	NAME.	ADDRESS.	AMOUNT.
1914.			
Aug. 7th	John Roach	Brechin	$25 00
" 30th	John E. McLean	Orillia	25 00
Sept. 4th	James Richardson	Noelville	25 00
" 22nd	Adrien Bonin	Bonfield	25 00
Oct. 1st	A. T. Colville	Mitchell	50 00
" 15th	H. Schofield	Toronto	25 00
Nov. 5th	Georges Dupont	Ottawa	25 00
Dec. 14th	Julius Weichels	Stratford	50 00
1915.			
Jan. 21st	Elizabeth Henn	Toronto	25 00
" 21st	J. Ward	Toronto	25 00
" 30th	L. G. Hodder	White River	25 00
" 30th	J. E. Merritt	Huntsville	30 00
Mar. 6th	W. S. Hodgins	Fort William	40 00
" 16th	C. H. Granger	Toronto	25 00
" 16th	J. W. Black	Toronto	25 00
" 20th	Elizabeth Lumb	Runnymede	25 00
" 25th	Angelina Curto	Hamilton	25 00
Apr. 26th	J. A. MacDonald	Delhi	25 00

$520 00

Expenses, 1914-1915.

June 6th—W. D. Child for copy of evidence re Schofield.... $1 00
   17th—Fare to Brechin and return 3 60
   17th—Hotel at Brechin 1 00
   20th—Fare to Thorold and return 1 30
   20th—Hotel bill at Thorold 50
   22nd—Paid C. C. Att. Kerr, Cobourg, for copy of
        evidence re Dr. McArthur 9 17

$16 57

Aug. 4th—Railway fare to Brechin and return 3 60
   5th—Railway fare Brechin to Orillia and return........ 60
   7th—Hotels at Brechin and Orillia, three days........... 6 00
   17th—Railway fare to Sudbury 7 70
   17th—Railway fare Sudbury to Sturgeon Falls........ 1 70
   19th—Boat fare Sturgeon Falls to Monteville and
        return 2 00
   20th—Railway fare Sturgeon Falls to Warren and
        return 1 00
   20th—Railway fare Sturgeon Falls to North Bay........ 65
   20th—Railway fare North Bay to Bonfield and return 1 00

21st—Railway fare North Bay to Toronto	6	80
21st—Hotel bills five days, at $2.00 per day	10	00
27th—Paid Dominic Depsqule re Ontario Medical Institute	1	00
	$42	05

Sept.	18th—Paid to find witness re Dr. Turofsky	1	00
	21st—Railway fare to Stratford	2	65
	21st—Railway fare Stratford to Mitchell and return		70
	21st—Railway fare Stratford to Toronto	2	65
	21st—Hotel bill at Stratford	1	00
	22nd—Paid Police Court Clerk for copy of evidence re Dr. Adams	1	00
	30th—Railway fare to Stratford	2	65
	30th—Hotel bill at Stratford		35
	30th—Railway fare Stratford to Mitchell and return		70
Oct.	1st—Hotel bill at Mitchell	2	00
	1st—Railway fare Stratford to Ingersoll		95
	1st—Paid Dr. Cornish for consultation and medicine	1	00
	2nd—Hotel bill at Ingersoll	2	30
	2nd—Railway fare Ingersoll to Toronto	2	90
	10th—Paid to Dr. Lapenta, Hamilton, for consultation and medicine	1	00
	13th—Railway fare to Ottawa and return	16	35
	14th—Hotel bill at Ottawa	2	00
	20th—Railway fare to Hamilton and return	1	95
	21st—Hotel bill at Hamilton	2	00
		$45	15

Nov.	12th—Paid Police Court Clerk, Toronto, for three copies of convictions re Dr. C. W. Walker	3	00
	21st—Paid Mary O'Neill conduct money as witness for Discipline Committee, re Dr. Turofsky	1	00
		$4	00

	30th—Railway fare to St. Catharines and return	3	60
	30th—Hotel bill at St. Catharines	1	00
Dec.	3rd—Railway fare to Hamilton and return	1	95
	3rd—Railway fare Hamilton to St. Catharines, and return and bus	1	95
	3rd—Hotel bills at St. Catharines and Hamilton	1	00
	7th—Paid F. G. Heal for services re J. Ward	2	00
	7th—Examination of Heal and medicine re J. Ward		50
	11th—Paid Wm. Beverley for services re J. Ward	1	50
	11th—Examination of Beverley and medicine re J. Ward	1	00

23rd—Paid F. G. Heal as witness re J. Ward 2 00
23rd—Paid Wm. Beverley as witness re J. Ward........ 1 50

$18 00

Jan. 6th—Paid six witnesses conduct money re Discipline
              Committee ....: 6 00
      10th—Railway fare to White River, re L. G. Hodder.... 16 85
      10th—Sleeper to Sudbury 1 75
      11th—Railway fare White River to Port Arthur and
              return re W. S. Hodgins 12 45
      11th—Sleeper White River to Port Arthur 1 25
      12th—Car fare and telephone at Port Arthur and Fort
              William 25
      13th—Sleeper White River to Sudbury 1 50
      13th—Railway fare White River to Parry Sound re
              S. B. Biehn 12 35
      15th—Stage, railway and bus fare Parry Sound to
              Huntsville re J. E. Merritt 2 45
      15th—Livery rig interviewing witnesses 1 50
      16th—Railway fare Huntsville to Toronto 4 40
      18th—Hotels and meals for five days 10 35
      18th—Paid Provincial Secretary's Office for informa-
              tion re Merritt 25

$71 35

Feb. 3rd—Paid W. G. Beverley witness Discipline Com-
              mittee re Dr. Walker 1 50
      6th—Paid S. J. Massey, witness Discipline Committee
              re Dr. Adams 1 00
      8th—Taxi Cab, Ltd., conveying Maud Fryday to and
              from Discipline Committee, witness re Dr.
              Adams 3 00
      8th—Paid Emile Hilpert, witness Discipline Com-
              mittee re Dr. Walker 2 00
      9th—Paid Mary O'Neill, witness Discipline Com-
              mittee re Dr. Turofsky 1 00
      13th—Paid W. G. Beverley, consultation and medicine
              re C. H. Granger 2 00
      15th—Paid W. G. Beverley for services re C. H.
              Granger 1 50
      22nd—Paid Wm. Hannigan for services re C. H.
              Granger 1 50
      22nd—For consultation and medicine 1 00
      24th—W. G. Beverley, witness fee re C. H. Granger 1 50
      24th—Wm. Hannigan, witness fee re C. H. Granger.... 1 50

24th—Wm. G. Beverley for services re J. W. Black....   1 50
For consultation and medicine 1 00
24th—Wm. Hannigan for services re J. W. Black........   1 50
For consultation and medicine 1 00

        $22 50

Mar. 2nd—Paid Wm. Hannigan, witness fee re J. W. Black   2 00
3rd—Railway fare to Brechin and return re John
     Roach 3 60
3rd—Rig to Justice of Peace to lay information 1 50
3rd—Hotel at Brechin and meal at Blackwater 1 00
5th—Fare to Hamilton and return 1 95
6th—Hotel at Hamilton $2.00, street car fare 25c.....   2 25
8th—Paid W. G. Beverley, witness fee re J. W. Black   1 50
11th—Railway fare to Brighton and return 4 75
12th—Hotel and bus at Brighton and Colborne 2 50
15th—Railway fare to Brechin and return 3 60
    Hotel at Brechin and meal at Blackwater........   1 00
17th—Railway fare to Hamilton and return 1 95
18th—Hotel $2.00, street car fare 25c. 2 25
22nd—Railway fare to Delhi and return 4 70
24th—Street car fares 25c., Hotels at Delhi and Hamil-
     ton, 2½ days, $5.00 ....   5 25

        $39 80

Apr. 7th—Paid H. Baker, Hamilton for services re Mrs.
     Curto 2 00
22nd—Paid M. O'Donnell, J.P., for copy of evidence
     re J. Roach 1 00

        $3 00

Total Expenses $262 42
Total Receipts $520 00

On the suggestion of the President the rules of order were suspended for the remainder of the session.

Dr. King moved, seconded by Dr. Stewart, the following motion, of which notice was given at an earlier session:

That it be an instruction to the Registrar to prepare a circular letter, setting out the fact that a Register exists, that an annual fee is payable to the College, that unless change of address is forwarded to the College, disadvantages to the Licentiates may accrue, that to insure his franchise, the correctness of the Register is essential, and any other information that a recent licentiate should know.

The President put the motion, which, on a vote having been taken, was declared carried.

The following motion was put by the President and on a vote having been taken, was declared carried:

Moved by Dr. Spankie, seconded by Dr. Crain, that whereas it has become known to the members of this Council of the College of Physicians and Surgeons of Ontario, that many of our soldiers in Europe are now suffering in special ways from various forms of nervous and mental trouble due to the terrible shock of war, and,

Whereas these various forms of nervous and mental diseases require special treatment and that efforts are being put forth by those in authority to give this special treatment so far as the circumstances and conditions of war permit, nevertheless these circumstances and conditions are such as to render adequate treatment impossible, and in consequence many of our brave young men are not receiving the care and chance for life and health which properly specialized and experienced medical treatment and nursing might give them, therefore be it resolved that this Council respectfully but urgently request the Government of this Province of Ontario to at once equip an expedition of experienced and specially trained physicians and nurses from its public institutions and others specially qualified for such work and despatch them without delay with proper and full equipment to minister to those afflicted and restore them to convalescence and health, or where this is impossible or likely to be unduly prolonged, to request the War Office to send them home to Canada when suitable accommodation, such as that soon available at Whitby, be prepared for their reception, and that this special treatment and nursing be there continued so long as may be required under the favorable conditions that such location, surroundings and accommodations afford. And, that a copy of this resolution be sent to Hon. W. H. Hearst, Premier of Ontario.

Dr. Ryan moved, seconded by Dr. Spankie, that a vote of thanks be extended to the President, Dr. Griffin, by the Council, for the able and courteous manner in which he has conducted the proceedings of the meeting of the Council.

The Registrar put the motion, which, on a vote having been taken, was declared carried unanimously.

The Registrar read the minutes of the present session, which were confirmed and signed by the President.

There being no further business to come before the Council it was moved by Dr. Johnson, seconded by Dr. Ryan, that the Council do now adjourn.

The President put the motion, which, on a vote having been taken, was declared carried, and the Council adjourned at 11.30 o'clock a.m.

(Sgd.) H. S. GRIFFIN,
President.

July 2nd, 1915.

Board of Examiners—Spring, 1914.

Name	Retaining Fee	Oral Exam. Allowance	Travel Time Allowance	Mileage	Total
Dr. R. H. Arthur	$20.00	$307.50	$67.50	$54.50	$449.50
Dr. W. T. Connell	20.00	307.50	22.50	28.50	378.50
Dr. G. L. Husband	20.00	7.50	7.50	4.00	39.00
Dr. A. S. Lockhart	20.00	292.50	45.00	30.40	387.90
Dr. W. A. McFall	20.00	7.50	....	....	27.50
Dr. E. Seaborn	20.00	300.00	37.50	46.70	404.20
Dr. P. Stuart	20.00	262.50	45.00	42.65	370.15
Dr. W. B. Thistle	20.00	270.00	22.50	27.80	340.30

Board of Examiners—Fall, 1914.

Name	Retaining Fee	Examination Allowance	Travel Time Allowance	Mileage	Total
Dr. R. H. Arthur	$20.00	$120.00	$15.00	$52.40	$207.40
Dr. W. T. Connell	20.00	112.50	15.00	16.50	164.00
Dr. G. L. Husband	20.00	7.50	7.50	4.00	39.00
Dr. A. S. Lockhart	20.00	90.00	....	16.50	126.50
Dr. W. A. McFall	20.00	7.50	....	....	27.50
Dr. E. Seaborn	20.00	105.00	15.00	18.75	158.75
Dr. P. Stuart	20.00	90.00	15.00	9.60	134.60
Dr. B. P. Watson	20.00	90.00	....	....	110.00

Legislation Committee, Meeting, March 16th, 1915.

Name	Attendance Allowance	Travel Time Allowance	Mileage	Total
Dr. E. E. King	$ 7.50	....	....	$ 7.50
Dr. J. Macarthur	15.00	$ 7.50	$12.00	34.50

Discipline Committee, Meeting Feb. 3rd, 1915.

Name	Attendance Allowance	Travel Time Allowance	Mileage	Total
Dr. W. E. Crain	$20.00	$40.00	$29.00	$89.00
Dr. A. T. Emmerson	20.00	10.00	13.40	43.40
Dr. A. E. Wickens	20.00	....	4.00	24.00
Dr. T. W. H. Young	20.00	20.00	25.60	65.60

Executive Committee Meetings.

Name	Attendance Allowance	Travel Time Allowance	Mileage	Total
Meeting, Sept. 29th, 1914—				
Dr. H. S. Griffin	$15.00	....	$ 4.00	$19.00
Dr. E. A. P. Hardy	7.50	....	....	7.50
Dr. J. Macarthur	15.00	....	12.00	27.00
Meeting, Oct. 29th, 1914—				
Dr. H. S. Griffin	15.00	....	4.00	19.00
Dr. J. Macarthur	15.00	$7.50	12.00	34.50
and by request:—				
Dr. W. L. T. Addison	7.50	....	....	7.50
Dr. A. J. Johnson	7.50	....	....	7.50
Dr. E. E. King	7.50	....	....	7.50
Meeting, Nov. 25th, 1915—				
Dr. H. S. Griffin	15.00	....	4.00	19.00
Dr. E. A. P. Hardy	7.50	....	....	7.50
Dr. J. Macarthur	15.00	7.50	12.00	34.50
Meeting, March, 2nd, 1915—				
Dr. H. S. Griffin	15.00	....	4.00	19.00
Dr. E. A. P. Hardy	7.50	....	....	7.50
Dr. J. Macarthur	15.00	....	12.00	27.00
and by request:—				
Dr. E. E. King	7.50	....	....	7.50
Meeting, April 2nd, 1915—				
Dr. H. S. Griffin	15.00	....	4.00	19.00
Dr. E. A. P. Hardy	7.50	....	....	7.50
Dr. J. Macarthur	15.00	....	12.00	27.00
and by request:—				
Dr. E. E. King	7.50	....	....	7.50

Special Council Meeting—December, 1914.

Name	Sessional Allowance	Travel Time Allowance	Mileage	Total
Dr. W. L. T. Addison	$50.00	....	....	$ 50.00
Dr. J. F. Argue	50.00	$40.00	$25.60	115.60
Dr. R. H. Arthur	50.00	40.00	26.20	116.20
Dr. H. Becker	50.00	....	....	50.00
Dr. G. M. Brodie	50.00	20.00	8.80	78.80
Dr. W. E. Crain	50.00	60.00	29.00	139.00
Dr. G. R. Cruickshank	50.00	30.00	22.80	102.80
Dr. F. A. Dales	50.00	20.00	2.90	72.90
Dr. A. T. Emmerson	50.00	20.00	13.40	83.40
Dr. T. S. Farncomb	50.00	20.00	10.10	80.10
Dr. R. Ferguson	50.00	20.00	12.00	82.00
Dr. H. S. Griffin	50.00	20.00	4.00	74.00
Dr. H. J. Hamilton	50.00	....	....	50.00

Name	Sessional Allowance	Travel Time Allowance	Mileage	Total
Dr. E. A. P. Hardy	50.00	....	....	50.00
Dr. C. E. Jarvis	50.00	20.00	12.00	82.00
Dr. A. J. Johnson	50.00	....	....	50.00
Dr. E. T. Kellam	30.00	20.00	8.20	58.20
Dr. E. E. King	50.00	....	....	50.00
Dr. J. Macarthur	50.00	20.00	12.00	82.00
Dr. J. M. MacCallum	50.00	....	....	50.00
Dr. S. McCallum	50.00	20.00	10.70	80.70
Dr. G. A. Routledge	50.00	20.00	12.10	82.10
Dr. E. Ryan	50.00	40.00	16.50	106.50
Dr. W. Spankie	50.00	40.00	16.50	106.50
Dr. A. D. Stewart	50.00	80.00	81.50	211.50
Dr. J. J. Walters	50.00	20.00	6.25	76.25
Dr. A. E. Wickens	50.00	20.00	4.00	74.00
Dr. T. W. H. Young	50.00	20.00	7.60	77.60

COUNCIL MEETING—JULY, 1914.

Name	Sessional Allowance	Travel Time Allowance	Mileage	Total
Dr. W. L. T. Addison	$100.00	....	....	$100.00
Dr. H. Bascom	100.00	$20.00	$ 3.00	123.00
Dr. H. Becker	100.00	....	....	100.00
Dr. W. E. Crain	100.00	40.00	29.00	169.00
Dr. G. R. Cruickshank	100.00	40.00	22.80	162.80
Dr. A. T. Emmerson	100.00	20.00	13.40	133.40
Dr. R. Ferguson	100.00	20.00	12.00	132.00
Dr. R. J. Gibson	100.00	40.00	44.40	184.40
Dr. Sir James Grant	100.00	40.00	25.60	165.60
Dr. H. S. Griffin	100.00	10.00	4.00	114.00
Dr. E. A. P. Hardy	100.00	....	....	100.00
Dr. J. S. Hart	100.00	....	....	100.00
Dr. C. E. Jarvis	100.00	20.00	12.00	132.00
Dr. A. J. Johnson	100.00	....	....	100.00
Dr. J. Macarthur	100.00	30.00	12.00	142.00
Dr. A. E. MacColl	100.00	20.00	11.40	131.40
Dr. J. M. MacCallum	100.00	——	——	100.00
Dr. S. McCallum	100.00	20.00	10.70	130.70
Dr. W. H. Merritt	100.00	20.00	....	120.00
Dr. G. A. Routledge	100.00	20.00	12.10	132.10
Dr. E. Ryan	100.00	20.00	16.50	136.50
Dr. W. Spankie	100.00	40.00	16.50	156.50
Dr. A. D. Stewart	100.00	80.00	81.50	261.50
Dr. T. W. Vardon	100.00	20.00	5.70	125.70
Dr. A. B. Welford	100.00	20.00	8.80	128.80
Dr. A. E. Wickens	100.00	10.00	4.00	114.00
Dr. T. W. H. Young	100.00	20.00	7.60	127.60

TREASURER'S REPORT.

To the Members of the Council of the College of Physicians and
Surgeons of Ontario:

Gentlemen,—I beg to submit herewith Financial Statement for
the Council Year, 1914-1915, just ended.

RECEIPTS.

Balance in Bank, June 30th, 1914, as audited		$19,051 45
Assessment Dues—		
Collected by Registrar	$2,510 00	
Collected by Bank	2,672 00	
		5,182 00
Registration Fees		3,280 00
Fines		520 00
Examination Fees—		
Fall Exam., 1914	$ 2,405 00	
Spring Exam., 1915	10,510 00	
		12,915 00
Registration Fees of applicants for Ontario License, qualifying under Dominion Medical Council Certificates		1,500 00
Fees of Ontario Council Licentiates, for Certificates of standing, when applying to the Dominion Medical Council		70 00
Fees of Ontario Council Registrants, for Certificates of standing, when applying to the Dominion Medical Council		550 00
Fees from rejected Candidates, whose appeals for examination standing have not been granted by the Council		40 00
Fee from Licentiate of the College, asking to be transferred from the General to the Homoeopathic Register		2 00
Interest on Bonds		1,000 00
Interest on Current Bank Account		324 52
		$44,434 97

Expenditures.

Council Meeting, July, 1914—
Members' allowance $3,623 00
Stenographic report of proceedings, etc.... 105 00
───────── $3,728 00
Council Meeting—
December, 1914 ....$2,332 15
Page at meeting 2 50
───────── 2,334 65
Officers' Salaries—
Registrar $2,750 00
Treasurer 700 00
Prosecutor 1,200 00
───────── 4,650 00
Legal services, general 302 82
Prosecutions: Legal charges, witness fees, court fees,
travelling expenses, etc. 271 33
Executive Committee 312 50
Legislation Committee 42 00
Discipline Committee 222 00
Discipline procedure 136 25
Printing Examination Papers, Diplomas, etc. 603 60
Printing Annual Announcement 473 30
Telephone service 143 60
Holding Professional Examinations—
General Expenses $273 70
Examiners' Fees, etc.—
Spring Exam., 1914 ....$2,397 05
Fall Exam., 1914 .... 967 75
───────── 3,364 80
───────── 3,638 50
Fees refunded to students, who did not take exams........ 200 00
Audit of Treasurer's and Registrar's books, vouchers,
etc. 75 00
Rental of Safety Deposit Box (for safekeeping of bonds) 3 00
Registrar's Office—Supplies, etc. (This item includes
postage, $456.73, on announcements, assessment
notices, etc.) 504 33
Stenographer in Registrar's Office 780 00
Treasurer's bonds 30 00
Prosecutor's bond 5 00
Stenographer's bond 10 00
Treasurer's office expenses 15 00
Bank charges, re collection of assessment dues 149 37
Council elections 200 00
Rose, Miss J. A., Honorarium voted by Council 100 00
Construction of vault 270 00

Property and Building Maintenance—

Caretaking	$120 00		
Painting, Plumbing, Carpentering, etc.	170 49		
Electric light	8 41		
Gas	45 92		
Fuel	188 50		
Water	18 48		
Fire insurance	41 85		
		593 65	
Miscellaneous		332 30	
Balance in Bank, June 16th, 1915		24,308 77	
		$44,434 97	

All of which is respectfully submitted,

H. WILBERFORCE AIKINS,
Treasurer.

Having audited the books and accounts of the Treasurer of the College of Physicians and Surgeons of Ontario, including Bank and Cash Books, and Vouchers thereto, for the Council Year 1914-1915, I hereby certify that I find the same correct and complete, and that the above Statement of Receipts and Expenditures agrees therewith.

JAMES F. LAWSON, Chartered Accountant,
Auditor.

Toronto, June 21st, 1915.

INDEX

Page

Absence from Province, with relief from payment of assessment dues 91
Acting Secretary, at Annual Meeting, 1915 (Dr. A. D. Stewart) 109
Adams, Dr. W. M., 115, 122, 123, 140
Adjournment of Council—
Special Meeting, December, 1914 108
Annual Meeting, 1915 145
Announcement, for year 1915-1916 14
Annual Fee, due from College Members—
Amount of 24
By-law to levy same 92
Annual Meeting—
Date and place of, By-law governing 75
Annual Meeting of Council for 1915—
By-law providing for same (passed at Special Meeting, December, 1914) 102
Annual Meeting of Council for 1916—
By-law providing for same 93
Annual Meeting of Council for 1915—
Proceedings of same 109
Appeal for Reinstatement—
Dr. H. E. Sheppard.... 115, 134
Appeals for Reconsideration of Examination Standing—
Entertained only, when lodged anterior to next succeeding Council Meeting..25, 131
Fee to accompany Appeal. 25
Fee refunded, where Appeal granted 25, 131
Referred to Committee (at Special Meeting, December, 1914) 99
with Committee's recommendations 107
Referred to Committee (at Annual Meeting, 1915) 112, 114, 116, 117
with Committee's recommendations 117, 126

Page

Appeals for Refund of Fees, etc.—
referred to Finance Committee 112, 115
with Committee's recommendations 131
Army Medical Corps, special licenses re same 117, 132
Arrears of Assessment Dues—
Enquiry re 116, 119, 125
Assembling and Preserving By-laws, By-law governing 74
Assessment Dues—
Absence from Province relieves from payment 91
Annual amount of 24
Arrears (enquiry) ..116, 119, 125
By-law to levy 92
Auditor— .
Report of, read and referred to Finance Committee 115
Belgian Relief Fund...115, 130, 131
Board of Examiners—
(See Examiners).
Bray, Dr. J. L., Registrar—
Resignation of 110, 122
Retiring allowance to..122, 131
British Pharmacopoeia, and College of Pharmacy 112, 127
British Registration—
(See also Reciprocity).
Fees re same 25
Requirements, to register in Ontario 19, 129
By-laws—
Adopted (Special Meeting, December, 1914) 101
Adopted (Annual Meeting), upon recommendation of Rules and Regulations Committee 134
How to proceed to draft same, By-law governing ... 81
re Absence of Members from Province, with relief from payment of assessment dues—By-law No. 8 91
re Annual Assessment Dues, to levy same—By-law No. 9 92

Page

re Annual and Special Meetings, calling of same—By-law No. 3 75

re Annual Meeting for 1915, fixing date and place (passed at Special Meeting, December, 1914)—By-law No. 12 102

re Annual Meeting for 1916, date and place of—By-law No. 12 93
also By-law No. 3 75

re Assembling and preserving By-laws—By-law No. 2 74

re Committee on Discipline, appointment and composition of, (passed at Special Meeting, December, 1914) By-law No. 10 101

re Committee on Discipline, appointment and composition of (passed at Annual Meeting, 1915) By-law No. 10 92

re Election of Homeopathic Members—By-law No. 6.... 87

re Election to Division No. 3—By-law No. 5 83

re Examinations (time, manner, places of) and Examiners (appointment of)—By-law No. 7 90

re Examiners, appointed to act from January to July, 1915 (passed at Special Meeting, December, 1914)—By-law No. 7 103

re Executive Committee, appointment and composition of (passed at Special Meeting, December, 1914)—By-law No. 11 101

re Executive Committee, appointment and composition of (passed at Annual Meeting, 1915)—By-law No. 11.. 93

re Legislative Committee, appointment and composition of (passed at Special Meeting, December, 1914)—By-law No. 13 102

re Legislative Committee, appointment and composition of (passed at Annual Meeting, 1915)—By-law No. 13 94

re Payment of Council Members, Members of Commit-

Page

tees, Examiners, Officers, etc., etc.—By-law No. 4.... 82

re Permanency of form of By-laws—By-law No. 14... 94

re Repealing existing By-laws—By-law No. 1 74

re Rules and Regulations, for conducting Council Proceedings—By-law No. 3... 75

Canada Medical Council—
(See Dominion Medical Council).

Canadian Expeditionary Forces, and licenses granted in connection with same 117

Canadian Soldiers in Europe, suffering from nervous or mental conditions, due to shock. Resolution (Spankie), suggesting measures for relief of same, to be forwarded to Premier of Ontario 145

Changes in Curriculum—
When to take effect 15

Chiropractic Methods, etc., referred to Executive Committee, for investigation 136

Circular Letter to College Members, inviting co-operation in preparing new Register. 144

College Members—
By Examination, since issue of last Register 33
Otherwise, than by examination 56
Names of, omitted from last published Register 56
Circular letter to, re new Register 144

College Officers—
For current year, 1915-1916 9

College of Mano-Therapy—
Communication from 119
Education Committee's recommendation 127

College of Pharmacy—
re Use of British Pharmacopoeia 112, 127

Colville, A. T.—
re College of Mano-Therapy 119, 127

Commission, Royal— ... ...
(See Royal Commission).

Committee of the Whole—
Rules governing its conduct 80

Page

Committees (and composition
of)—
Complaints, Discipline, Education, Executive, Finance,
Legislative, Printing, Property, Registration, Rules
and Regulations 10
(See each Committee, under
its own appropriate head-
ing).
on Credentials (of Council
Members, at Special Meet-
ing, December, 1914) 95
Duties of, as defined by By-
law 81
Payment of, By-law govern-
ing 82
President and Vice-Presi-
dent, members of all Com-
mittees, save Discipline and
Executive 76
Standing Committees requir-
ed by By-law 76
(See also under Standing
Committees).
Committee on Discipline—
(See under Discipline Com-
mittee).
Committee on Education—
. (See under Education Com-
mittee).
Committees, Special—
(See under Special Commit-
tees).
Committees, Standing—
(See under Standing Com-
mittees).
Communications—
(See under Appeals).
Complaints Committee—
' Appeals referred to Com-
mittee (Special Meeting,
December, 1914) 99
Report of, containing recom-
mendations re same 107
Appeals referred to Com-
mittee (Annual Meeting,
1915) 112, 114, 116
Report of, re appeals for
standing, read and adopted 126
Selection of, December, 1914 '99
Selection of, June, 1915.... 112
Convener of Committee—
December, 1914 99
June, 1915 112
Council—
Annual Meeting, date and

Page

place of, By-law govern-
ing 75, 93, 102
Annual Meeting, 1915, proceedings of 109
Annual Meeting, 1916, date
and place of, under By-law 93
Membership of, 1914 95
Membership of, 1915 7
Indemnity to members fixed
by resolution, (Special
Meeting, December, 1914). 106
Indemnity to members, (Annual Meeting, 1915), By-law
governing 82
Interval Meeting, held subsequent to General Election,
newly elected Council qualifies, (opinion, H. S. Osler,
K.C.) 97
Officers required, and how
elected, By-law governing. 75
Officers for Council year,
1915-1916 9
Officers, election of, at Special Meeting, 1914 .... 96, 98
at Annual Meeting, 1915 .. 109
Organization of, By-law
governing 76
Payments made to members
(at Special and Annual
Meetings), given in de-
tail 148, 149
Powers of 14
Rules and Regulations, for con-
ducting proceedings of, By-
law governing 75
Rules of Order, By-law
governing 76
Special Meeting (Decem-
ber, 1914), proceedings ... 95
Credentials Committee—
re Council Members, Special
Meeting, December, 1914 .. 95
Report of same 95
Cruickshank, Dr. G. R.—
Enquiries re Royal Commis-
sion 120
Curriculum—
Changes in same, when to
take effect 15
Homoeopathic 19
Requirements of 16
Special Committee appoint-
ed, to consider changes in 127
Degrees, Titles, etc.—
Registration of 24
Diploma—
Fee for same 24

Page

Discipline Committee—
By-law appointing, (Special
Meeting, December, 1914). 101
By-law appointing, (Annual
Meeting. 1915) 92
Continuity of Service of.. 92
Payment of Members, By-
law governing 82
Payments made to members
during Council Year, 1914-
1915, given in detail 147
Reports of
re Adams, W. M., Turofsky,
H. A., and Walker, C. W.,
presented 115
Report re W. M. Adams, as
read and adopted......122, 123
Report re H. E. Sheppard, as
adopted 134
Report re H. A. Turofsky,
as read and adopted...123, 124
Report re C. W. Walker,
adoption moved, but re-
ferred to later Session 123
Adopted in Council 133
Division No. 3—
By-law re election to same 83
Dominion Medical Council—
Fee for enabling certificate 24
Gibson, Dr. R. J. (President
D. M. C.), addresses Council 120
Officers of, for 1915-1916.. 121
re Reciprocity 121
Report of Representatives
to, presented. read and
adopted 119, 120
Education Committee—
Report of, recommending
Examiners from January to
July, 1915 (passed at Spec-
ial Meeting, December,
1914) 103
Report of, (Annual Meeting,
1915)—
Presented 119, 124
Read and adopted 126
Report itself 127
Selection of, December, 1914 99
Selection of, June, 1915.. 112
Education, Medical—
Uniform Standards, (Re-
port re Dominion Medical
Council) 121
Election, Division No. 3—
By-law governing 83
Election—
Homeopathic, By-law gov-
erning 87

Page

of New Council (opinion of
H. S. Osler, K.C.) 97
of officers, By-law govern-
ing 75
of officers, Special Meeting.
December, 1914 96-98
Annual Meeting, 1915 109
Voting paper, form of 87
Enabling Legislation—
re Reciprocity 98-105
Enquiries—
re Medical Register, and
members in arrears 116
re Royal Commission 120
Entrance to Rear of Property.. 138
Evidence, to be collected for
Royal Commission 119, 125
Examiners—
Appointment of, under By-
law 90
Appointment for period
January to July, 1915 (at
Special Meeting, December,
1914) 103
Appointed for 1915-1916 (at
Annual Meeting, 1915) ... 127
Composition of Board 9
Duties of 20
Homeopathic, names and
subjects 90
(See also under heading
Homeopathic).
Names of, with subjects al-
lotted to, under By-law 90
Payment of, By-law govern-
ing 83
Payments made to Board of
Examiners (given in detail) 147
Examinations—
Appeals from Examination
returns, fee re same 25
By-law providing for 90
Date, place and require-
ments of 20
Date and place of Fall Ex-
amination. 1915 90
Date and places of Spring
Examination, 1916 90
Duties of Registrar and
Board of Examiners 21
Fees payable for same 24
Homoeopathic, requirements
of 20
Homoeopathic Examination
questions and answers 23
Papers, set at Fall Examina-
tion, 1914 26
at Spring Examination, 1915 29

Page

Papers, Homeopathic, set
at Fall Examination, 1914.   28
set at Spring Examination,
1915 31
Report, embracing results of
Fall Examinations, 1914,
and Spring Examinations,
1915, read by President and
adopted 113
Rules for guidance of candidates 22

Executive Committee—
Appeals for standing 117
By-law appointing, (passed
at Special Meeting, Decem-
ber, 1914) ....:..... 101
By-law appointing (passed
at Annual Meeting, 1915). 93
Licenses granted by 117
Payment of, By-law govern-
ing 82
Payments made to members
of, (given in detail) 148
Report of, read and adopted 116

Farm, Sanitation of the—
(Sir James Grant) 137

Fees 24

Finance Committee—
Amendments re Sessional
Indemnity 106, 130
Appeals for refund of fees,
etc. 112, 115
re Belgian Relief Fund
115, 130, 131
Report presented (Special
Meeting, December, 1914). 104
Report discussed and adopt-
ed (Special Meeting, De-
cember,.1914) 106
Report, motion to adopt... 130
and Amendment, increasing
gift to Belgian Relief Fund
(Annual Meeting, 1915) ... 130
Report itself, as adopted.. 130
Selection of, December, 1914 99
Selection of, June, 1915... 111
General Orders of the Day..... 78
Gibson, Dr. R. J. (President
Dom. Med. Council), ad-
dresses Council 120
Graduates in Medicine—
Of non-Canadian Colleges,
h: w to qualify 19
Grant, Sir James—
Motion, re Infant Life..113-115
Motion, re Sanitation of the
Farm..................... 137

Page

Great Britain, Reciprocity with—
(See under Reciprocity).
Homeopathic—
Curriculum 19
Candidates   for   Examina-
tion 20-23
Elections, By-law govern-
ing 87
Examiners, how selected.. 20
Examination papers,
Fall, 1914 .... 2S
Spring, 1915 ....:.. 31
Examinations, By-law pro-
viding for same 90
Voting paper, form of 89
Honorarium—
To Miss J. A. Rose 137
Indemnity, Sessional—
By-law governing payment
of same 82
Finance Committee's recom-
mendation   re   same   (An-
nual Meeting, 1915) 131
Resolution   fixing   amount
(Special Meeting, Decem-
ber, 1914) 106
Infant Life Mortality—
Motion   re,   (Sir   James
Grant) 113-115
Introduction of By-laws 81
Kingston Medical and Surgical
Association—
re Reciprocity 99
Koljonen, Dr.—
referred to Executive Com-
mittee 105, 107
Legal Advice, H. S. Osler, K.C.—
Opinion — Council,   newly
elected, subsequent to An-
nual Meeting, constitutes
Council at Interval Meeting,
following Election 97
Reciprocity with United
Kingdom, how to proceed to
obtain same, (Address, Spec-
ial   Meeting,   December,
1914) 99
Legislation, Medical—
Canadian Medical Associa-
tion's attitude towards ... 121
Enabling clause,. re Reci-
procity 98-105
Legislative Committee—
By-law appointing, and com-
position of, for 1914-1915,
(passed at Special Meeting,
December, 1914) 102
By-law appointing, and com-

Page

position of, for 1915-1916, (passed at Annual Meeting, 1915) 94

Medical Education and Practice, referred to Legislative Committee 105

Payment of Members, By-law governing 82

Payments made to members of (given in detail) 147

Reciprocity issue. referred to Legislative Committee for elaboration, etc. (Special Meeting, December, 1914). 105

Report of, re Reciprocity with Great Britain, presented (at Annual Meeting, 1915) 116

Read and discussed 118

Adopted in Council 128

Licenses, Special—
(See also Special Licenses).
Granted, re Overseas Service 117

Licentiates—
By Examination, since issue of last Register 33

Otherwise, than by Examination 56

Names of, omitted from last Register 56

Macarthur, Dr. James—
(Deceased).
Presidential address of, at Special Meeting, December, 1914 96

Resolution expressing profound sorrow 111

Mano-Therapy, College of—
(See College of Mano-Therapy).

Matriculation—
Appeals for matriculation standing 104, 117, 132, 133

Fee for registration of.... 24

Requirements 16

Special Committee, re uniform standard of matriculation in the different Provinces 127

Medical Council of Ontario—
(See under Council).

Medical Council of Canada—
(See Dominion Medical Council).

Medical Commission—
Evidence to be colected for same 125

Page

Medical Curriculum—
(See under Curriculum).

Medical Education—
Motion to refer questions affecting Medical Education and Practice to Legislative Committee 105

Uniform standards of, (Report re Dom. Med. Council) 121

Medical Legislation, and Canadian Medical Association.. 121

Medical Studies—
(See under Curriculum).

Meeting, Annual—
(See under Annual Meeting).

Meeting, Special, (December, 1914)—
(See under Special Meeting)

Members of College—
(See under College members).

Members of Council—
(See Council).

Motions, of which Notice Had Been Given—
(Special Meeting, December, 1914).
re Prosecutions Committee's Report 105

Motions, of which Notice Had Been Given—
(Annual Meeting, 1915).
re Evidence required for Royal Commission 125

re Honorarium to Miss J. A. Rose 137

re Infant Life Mortality .. 115

re License to Dr. H. Courtenay 137

re money grant, to promote investigation of methods, practices, etc., of Osteopaths, et al 136

re New Register, with clause relative to delinquents.... 125

re New Register 136

re Public Health Act, amendment, where death follows attendance of unlicensed practitioners 120

re Register, and circular letter to College Members.. 144

re Sanitation of the Farm (Sir James Grant) 137

Newly Elected Council Qualifies, in interval between Council Annual Meetings .. 97

Page

Notices of Motion—
(Special Meeting, December, 1914).
re By-laws 100
re Prosecutions Committee
Report 100
Notices of Motion—
(Annual Meeting, 1915).
re Amendment to Public
Health Act, and unlicensed
practitioners 116
re Evidence required for
Royal Commission 119
re Honorarium to Miss
J. A. Rose 125
re Infant Mortality, (Sir
James Grant) 113
re Money Grant, to promote
investigation of methods,
practices, etc., of Osteopaths, et al 124
re New Register, with clause
relative to delinquents ... 119
re New Medical Register.. 125
re Overseas Service License
to H. Courtenay 125
re New Register, and circular letter to College Members 136
re Sanitation of the Farm,
(Sir James Grant) 125
Officers, Council—
Election of, for Special
Meeting 96, 98
for Annual Meeting 109
For current year, 1915-
1916 9
Method of Election, By-
law governing 75
Payment of, By-law govern-
ing 83
Officers required by By-law 75
Officers, Past—
Of the College 11
Orders of the Day 78
Organization of Council—
By-law governing 76
Osler, H. S., K.C.—
(See also under Legal ad-
vice).
Appointment of, as Counsel,
December, 1914 98
June, 1915 110
re Reciprocity, how to pro-
ceed, to procure same, De-
cember, 1914 99

Page

Osteopathic Methods, etc.—
Referred to Executive Com-
mittee for investigation... 136
Overseas Service—
Licenses granted, re same. 117
Papers, Examination—
Fall, 1914 26
Spring, 1915 29
Homoeopathic:
Fall, 1914 28
Spring, 1915 31
Payment of Council Members,
Examiners, Officers, Com-
mittees, etc.—
By-law governing 82
Permanency, Form and Num-
ber of By-laws—
By-law governing 94
Petitions—
,(See Appeals).
Pharmacy Act 112, 127
President and Vice-President
members of all Committees
save Discipline and Execu-
tive 76
Presidents, Past 11
Printing Committee—
Report of 138
Selection of, December, 1914 99
Selection of, June, 1915... 111
Property Committee—
Report presented, read and
adopted, with permission to
modify wording, and report
same later 135
Report, as re-worded 137
Selection of, December, 1914 99
Selection of, June, 1915... 112
Vault, authority to con-
struct and equip, etc....106, 137
Prosecutions Committee—
Report of, with attached
Annual Report of Prosecu-
tor 138
Prosecutor's Annual Report.... 139
Prosecutor's Receipts and Dis-
bursements, itemized 141
Public Health Act, and cases of
death following attendance
by unlicensed practition-
ers 116, 120
Quorum, of Committees—
By-law governing 76
Rear Entrance to Property.... 138
Reciprocity with the United
Kingdom—
(See also British Registra-
tion).

Page

Amenament, affirming principle, on basis of Registers of Great Britain and Ontario 104-105

Amendment to amendment, calling for plebiscite 103

Amendment to amendment, to consider and report at Annual Meeting 105

Discussion on 103, 105

Dominion Medical Council, views on 121

Enabling legislation 98-105

Motion, to affirm principle, with appointment of committee, (Special Meeting, December, 1914) 99

Motion, referring to Legislative Committee, to elaborate details, negotiate further, take legal advice, etc., and report to Annual Meeting, (Special Meeting, December, 1914) 105

Motion, approving of principle, (amendment, as substantive motion) 105

Osler, H. S., K.C., addresses Council, on procedure to obtain, (Special Meeting, December, 1914) 99

''Regulation,'' q.v. 129

Report on, by Legislative Committee, presented 116

read and discussed 118

adopted in Council 128

Special Meeting of Council, to consider same 97

University of Toronto, communication from 104

Register, New—
re circular letter to College Members, inviting their co-operation in preparation of 144

re delinquents 116, 119, 125

re preparation of, with list to each territorial representative of his constituents for correction 136

Registrar—
Acting as such, at Annual Meeting, (Dr. Bray being ill), Dr. A. D. Stewart 109

Motion, naming Special Committee, to report on appointing new Registrar ... 110

Report of Committee presented 119

Page

Amendment to 122

Report read and adopted... 122

Report itself 122

Resignation of Dr. J. L. Bray, Registrar 110

Retiring allowance 122, 131

Registrars, Past 13

Registrar-Treasurer, newly elected, Dr. H. Wilberforce Aikins 122

Registration, British—
(See under British Registration). .

Registration Committee—
Appeals, referred to, (Special Meeting, December, 1914) 99-104

Report of, presented and adopted, (Special Meeting, December, 1914) 106

Appeals, referred to, (Annual Meeting, 1915)....112, 114

Report of, presented 130

and adopted, (Annual Meeting, 1915) 131, 132, 133

Selection of, December, 1914 98

Selection of, June, 1915... 111

Registration of degrees or titles, etc..—
Fee for same 24

''Regulation,'' setting forth conditions required of British licentiates, to register in Ontario 129

Reinstatement, appeal or Dr. H. E. Sheppard 115, 134

Relief from Payment of Assessment dues—
By-law governing 91

Repealing By-laws—
By-law governing 74

Reports (Special Meeting, December, 1914)—.
of Finance Committee, presented 104

discussed and adopted 106

of Registration Committee 104; 106

Reports (Annual Meeting, 1915)—
Auditor's, presented and referred to Finance Committee 115

Complaints Committee, read and adopted 126

Discipline Committee, re Adams, W. M., Turofsky,

Page

II. A., and Walker, C. W.,
presented and read 115
and adopted 122, 123, 133
and re Sheppard, H. E.... 134
Education Committee, pre-
sented 119, 124
read and adopted..... 126, 127
re Examinations, Fall, 1914,
and spring, 1915 113
- Executive Committee, read
and adopted 116
Finance Committee ......:. 130
Legislation Committee, on.
Reciprocity with Great
Britain, presented 116
read and discussed 118
adopted in Council 128
Printing Committee, pre-
sented, read and adopted.. 138
Property Committee, pre-
sented, read and adopted,
with permission to re-word
and report later 135
Report itself ....: 137
Prosecutions Committee,
with attached Annual Re-
port of Prosecutor. 138
Prosecutor's Annual Report 139
Registration Committee—
presented 130
adopted 131, 132
Representatives to Domin-
ion Medical Council, report
of 119, 120
Rules and Regulations Com-
mittee, re By-laws—
presented 119
adopted 134
Special Committee, re Re-
gistrar—
presented 119
read and adopted 122
Representatives to Dominion
Medical Council—
Report presented 119
read and adopted 120
Returning Officers—
Payment for services, By-
law governing 86
Robinson, C. K., Tamworth.... 140
Rose, Miss J. A.—
Honorarium 137
Royal Commission—
Enquiries concerning 120
Collecting and assembling in-
formation and evidence, for
submission to 119, 125

Page

Rules and Regulations, Touch-
ing Council. Meetings—
By-law governing 75
Rules and Regulations Com-
mittee—
Report of Committee, re
By-laws, presented 119
read and adopted 134
Selection of, December, 1914 98
Selection of, June, 1915... 111
Rules of Order—
By-law governing 76
Rules of Order, Suspended—
At Special Meeting, Decem-
ber, 1914 (re By-laws) 100
At Special Meeting, De-
cember, 1914, to introduce
By-law re Examiners. and
Examinations 103
At Annual Meeting, 1915,
for remainder of Session.. 144
Safety Deposit Box—
Access to, authorized 131
Salaries, to be Paid to Officers 83
Sanitation of the Farm 137
Sessional Indemnity—
By-law. governing 82
Sheppard, Dr. H. E.—
Appeal for reinstate-
ment 115, 134
Soldiers, Canadian, in Europe—
(See Canadian Soldiers).
Spankie, Dr.'s Resolution—
re Canadian Soldiers, dis-
abled 145
Special Committees—
re Curriculum (Ferguson,
Ryan, J. M. MacCallum)... 127
re Matriculation (Ferguson,
Addison, Wickens) 127
re Registrar (Hardy, John-
son, James MacCallum.
Ryan, Ferguson, Addison,
Spankie, King, Cruick-
shank) 110, 119, 122
Special Licenses—
re Overseas Service... 117, 137
Views of Dominion Medical
Council, re granting of
same 121
Special Meeting of Council (De-
cember, 1914)—
Adjournment of 108
Calling of Special Meet-
ings, By-law governing 75
Officers, election of 96
Opinion of H. S. Osler, K.C.,
that recently newly elected

Page

Council constitutes Council, for meeting following election 97
Presidential Address (Dr. James Macarthur, now deceased) 96
Reasons for calling same .. 97
Standards, Uniform—
(See Uniform Standards).
Standing By-laws—
By-law, re permanency of form of same 94
Standing Committees—
Composition of, 1915 10
Required by By-law 76
Selection of, December, 1914 98
Selection of, June, 1915... 111
Stewart, Dr. A. D., Acting Secretary, Annual Meeting, 1915 109
Stinson, Dr. A. W. 112
Studies, Medical—
(See under Curriculum).
Suspension of Rules of Order—
(See under Rules of Order).
Treasurer's Annual Report 150
Treasurers, Past 13
Turofsky, Dr. H. A.—
115, 122, 123, 124, 140

Page

Uniform Standard of Matriculation—
Committee appointed 127
Uniform Standard of Medical Education—
(Report re Dominion Medical Council) 121
University of Toronto—
Communication re Reciprocity 104
Unlicensed Practitioners—
With death following attendance 116-120
Methods, practices, etc., to be investigated by Executive Committee 136
Vault, authority to construct and equip 106
Report of Property Committee. re same 137
Vice-Presidents, Past 12
Vote of Thanks—
To President 145
Voting Papers—
In Election to Council, form of 87
Homeopathic, form of 89
Walker, Dr. C. W.—
115, 122, 123, 133, 140
Young, Dr. T. H. W., and Sessional indemnity 131